The Temple of the Future Age

a study of the closing chapters of the Prophecy of Ezekiel

Peter J Southgate

ISBN   978-1-874508-52-6

Published by the **Dawn Book Supply**
5 Station Road, Carlton, Nottingham NG4 3AT

Printed and bound in Great Britain

Contents

Author's preface

My interest in the future temple as outlined in the closing chapters of the Prophecy of Ezekiel has been a lifelong one. It was heightened about forty years ago by a request to address a meeting where this topic was on the programme.

A closer study of the subject, begun at this time, led to the realisation that some existing interpretations of Ezekiel's description contained many fundamental problems. Eventually this study resulted in the views set out in this book.

The interpretation in the following pages is far from being completely original, but may help to clarify a section of Scripture that at first reading may seem somewhat intimidating. This book does not claim to be either authoritative or comprehensive, and certainly not dogmatic. It is put forward at the request of many who sought a more permanent record of the author's views, which were first published in *The Dawn Ecclesial Magazine*.

Thanks are due to Roy Toms, whose graphics skills readily transformed my amateurish diagrams into something approaching an art-form, and who prepared the work for printing.

Above all, praise is due to the One who has revealed His intentions for the earth and mankind through the work of the Lord Jesus, of which the revelation about Ezekiel's temple is a part.

P.J.S. November 2013

Abbreviations

The following indicate the various scriptural versions used:

KJV   The King James Version

LXX   The Septuagint Version

NIV   The New International Version

NKJV The New King James version

RSV   The Revised Standard Version

Unless otherwise shown, Bible quotations are from the KJV

Chapter 1 **Initial thoughts**

The description of a temple recorded in the final chapters of Ezekiel's prophecy has long fascinated Bible students. It is generally believed that it represents a structure that will be built in the Holy Land when Christ returns to set up the Kingdom of God. In the late 17th century the famous scientist and theologian Sir Isaac Newton sketched out his own understanding of what the structure would be like (copies of his notes and sketches can be viewed on the Jewish National and University Library website); and in the intervening years many studies of Ezekiel's temple have been made, with varying suggestions put forward. In Christadelphian circles a major study was published at the end of the 19th century, which was widely, though far from universally, accepted.

More recently, this subject has been studied again and, by request, we submitted our ideas to *The Dawn Ecclesial Magazine*. These studies are reproduced here. The approach that will be adopted is to let Scripture speak for itself, hoping that our readers will try to rid the mind of any preconceptions that would hinder an understanding of that message. We emphasise at the outset that what will be advanced is a personal view that has developed gradually over many years, and readily acknowledge that much remains to be elucidated.

Ever since the angelic vision was given to Ezekiel there has been a divergence of views as to its overall significance, let alone the details. These different approaches can be summarised as follows:

A post-restoration design

One view is that Ezekiel, in captivity in Babylon, was shown the temple that the Jews were to erect on their return to Jerusalem. If this was so, then why did not Zerubbabel and Joshua build a temple with these specifications on their return from captivity? There is no evidence that the one they built contained the distinctive features of the temple that Ezekiel saw. This can be deduced because this "second temple" was refurbished by Herod the Great to make the temple existing in New Testament times, but without altering the overall design of Zerubbabel's temple. This design is known from Josephus's detailed account and does not correspond to the temple seen by Ezekiel.

A symbolic building

At the other extreme is the view that the whole structure is symbolic. In the same way that Revelation describes a symbolic city coming down from heaven, having features and dimensions that can be clearly defined as applying to the future redeemed, so Ezekiel's temple is said to be an allegory of the spiritual temple of God that is a familiar feature of divine revelation.

If this were so, then each of the very specific arrangements and precise dimensions that Ezekiel was given should be capable of a spiritual application. In Revelation we can readily see the general significance of the dimension of the New Jerusalem: a perfect cube of 12,000 furlongs (Rev. 21.16). It indicates the perfection of the immortal state, based upon the hope of Israel and its twelve tribes. Another general analogy is that God's completed spiritual temple had as its foundation the work of the twelve apostles (v.14). But in Ezekiel's structure the immense number of precise measurements – ranging from five hundred cubits in some cases to only two in others – must surely indicate a literal structure. If all these measurements have only a spiritual application then it must open the door for some very far-fetched and speculative interpretations that could be said to savour of astrology rather than divine revelation.

We suggest that as much space is given to a detailed description of this temple, we are safe in assuming that it will be as literal as the tabernacle and the temple of Solomon, for which detailed measurements were also given. It may be that, as in the case of these two previous buildings, the structure and ceremonies of the future temple will have a symbolic significance, but this cannot be used as an argument against their literal existence.

It is also worth noting that Ezekiel had visions of two temples, one at the beginning of his ministry and the other towards the end. None would deny that the first vision of the temple that Ezekiel had seen, as described in chapters 8–11, was the literal temple at Jerusalem, to which the prophet was transported in *"the visions of God"* (8.3). But a close comparison of the features of the temple actually in existence in his day and the one he saw in the second vision in chapters 40–48 shows many identical features. The literal temple had gates, an inner court, an altar, a threshold, a porch and an east gate – all of which are duplicated in the latter vision. In the first vision the glory of God departed by way of the east gate and in the second it returned through a similar entrance. Clearly if the first vision referred to a literal temple the second has to also.

A literal future building

The most reasonable and generally accepted view is that Ezekiel saw in vision a temple that has yet to be built in Israel at the return of Jesus. As we will now see, there are very many references that predict such a structure being in existence at the time of the end. In view of the fact that in the past the dimensions and layout of God's literal "dwelling-places" were specifically given, then it could be expected that the same would apply to His future temple. In this series we will assume that this is so. Indeed, as we proceed, we suggest that any other scheme of interpretation will be seen to be ruled out.

Prophecies of a future temple

We commence our study by establishing that other Scriptures than Ezekiel predict that there will indeed be a temple in the Kingdom and that it will be located at Jerusalem. The psalmist, after speaking of the *"hill of God"* as *"the hill which God desireth to dwell in; yea, the LORD will dwell in it for ever"*, continues: *"Because of thy **temple at Jerusalem** shall kings bring presents unto thee"* (Psa. 68.16,29; bold type added for emphasis throughout). Joel predicts that: *"a fountain shall come forth of the **house of the LORD**, and shall water the valley of Shittim"* (3.18). Isaiah foretells that when *"the mountain of the **LORD's house** shall be established"* that *"out of Zion shall go forth the law, and the word of the LORD from Jerusalem"* (2.2–3). He later says that in this temple animals such as rams, *"shall come up with acceptance on mine altar, and I will glorify the **house of my glory"*** (Isa. 60.7). This glory will be enhanced by natural products: *"The glory of Lebanon shall come unto thee, the fir tree, the pine tree, and the box together, to beautify the place of **my sanctuary**; and I will make the place of my feet glorious"* (v.13). Indeed *"the glory of this **latter house** shall be greater than of the former, saith the LORD of hosts: and in this place will I give peace"* (Hag. 2.9).

Future animal sacrifices

The inference from some of these passages that animal sacrifices will be offered on an altar in this temple is confirmed by other predictions. Of some worshippers in the future temple it is foretold: *"Their burnt offerings and their sacrifices shall be accepted upon mine altar"* (Isa. 56.7). God promised the Levites that they would always have *"a man before me to offer burnt offerings, and to kindle meat offerings, and to do sacrifice continually"* (Jer. 33.18), and when *"HOLINESS UNTO THE LORD"* is in operation Zechariah says that *"the pots in the LORD's house shall be like the bowls before the altar"* (14.20).

The temple builder, "The BRANCH"

In the days of Zechariah, the high priest Joshua was displayed as a type of his future namesake, Jesus. Of Christ's future work we read: *"Thus speaketh the LORD of hosts, saying, Behold the man whose name is The BRANCH; and he shall grow up out of his place, and he shall build the temple of the LORD: even he shall build the temple of the LORD; and he shall bear the glory, and shall sit and rule upon his throne; and he shall be a priest upon his throne: and the counsel of peace shall be between them both … And they that are far off shall come and build in the temple of the LORD"* (Zech. 6.12–15). Thus the clear and widespread teaching of Scripture is that a temple for worship and sacrifice will yet be built in Jerusalem.

But who will be the worshippers and who will offer those animal sacrifices? This is what we address in the next chapter.

Chapter 2 The worshippers

Having, we trust, shown from Scripture that a new temple will be built in Jerusalem on Christ's return, we now consider the important question of who will worship there. There are many references to this, and we will look at virtually all of them. It is often thought that because the temple will be *"an house of prayer for all people"* (Isa. 56.7) it will of necessity be very large to accommodate visitors from all over the world, and that the facilities for offering sacrifices will be correspondingly extensive. But a closer examination of those passages suggests that this immediate impression may not be correct. Access may be more limited, and the offering of sacrifices restricted to a certain class.

So let us consider in detail those passages that have a bearing on the future temple worship. In all such studies we must recognise that our understanding is imperfect and it is not for us to predict with certainty the details of any future events.

A focal point for instruction and worship

First, the well-known passage in Isaiah 2.2–3: *"And it shall come to pass in the last days, that the mountain of the LORD'S house shall be established in the top of the mountains, and shall be exalted above the hills; and all nations shall flow unto it. And many people shall go and say, Come ye, and let us go up to the mountain of the LORD, to the house of the God of Jacob; and he will teach us of his ways, and we will walk in his paths: for out of Zion shall go forth the law, and the word of the LORD from Jerusalem."* Here is a general prediction that many of the world's inhabitants will visit Jerusalem for instruction in the ways of God. No mention is made here of temple worship, let alone sacrifices; but of course these are not excluded by this reference.

But Psalm 86 is more specific: *"All nations whom thou hast made shall come and worship before thee, O Lord; and shall glorify thy name"* (v.9). A related prediction is in Isaiah 66 (although the context probably implies that this application is limited to Israel): *"And it shall come to pass, that from one new moon to another, and from one sabbath to another, shall all flesh come to worship before me, saith the LORD"* (v.23). Although these two passages do not mention Jerusalem as the focus of the worship, in view of the reference in Isaiah 2 it would be reasonable to assume that they, too, refer to worship at that city rather than elsewhere.

Jeremiah contains a more specific prediction, this time mentioning Jerusalem: *"At that time they shall call Jerusalem the throne of the LORD; and all the nations shall be gathered unto it, to the name of the LORD, to Jerusalem: neither shall they walk any more after the imagination of their evil heart"* (3.17).

Thus the world will worship at the temple; but as yet there has been no reference to sacrificial offerings.

Keeping the Feast of Tabernacles

In addition to these general references to worship at Jerusalem there is the well-known passage in Zechariah: *"And it shall come to pass, that every one that is left of all the nations which came against Jerusalem shall even go up from year to year to worship the King, the LORD of hosts, and to keep the feast of tabernacles. And it shall be, that whoso will not come up of all the families of the earth unto Jerusalem to worship the King, the LORD of hosts, even upon them shall be no rain. And if the family of Egypt go not up, and come not, that have no rain; there shall be the plague, wherewith the LORD will smite the heathen that come not up to keep the feast of tabernacles"* (14.16–18).

At first sight this predicts that *"all the families of the earth"* will not only worship at Jerusalem but celebrate the Feast of Tabernacles there. But this phrase must be taken in conjunction with the earlier one that defines who these families are, namely: *"every one that is left of all the nations which came against Jerusalem"*. Thus it seems likely that *"all the nations"* here refers to all nations local to Israel rather than a global sense. Certainly, if the attack *"against Jerusalem"* mentioned here is the same as in Ezekiel 38, then every nation of the world is not included in this command to visit Jerusalem, for the attackers there are limited to specific nations. Also, the individual threat to Egypt, alone of the many other arid nations of the world, seems to confirm this suggestion.

Egypt and Assyria

There is a reference in Isaiah which states – as one would expect – that regathered Israel will worship at Jerusalem: *"Ye shall be gathered one by one, O ye children of Israel … and they shall come which were ready to perish in the land of Assyria, and the outcasts in the land of Egypt, and shall worship the LORD in the holy mount at Jerusalem"* (27.12-13).

This reference to Assyria and Egypt leads us to another passage, which throws light on the future relationship of Israel's neighbours to Jerusalem and worship in the temple. Whilst not explicitly stating the fact, it implies that these two nations will share in the future worship: *"And the LORD shall be known to Egypt, and the Egyptians shall know the LORD in that day, and shall do sacrifice and oblation; yea, they shall vow a vow unto the LORD, and perform it. And the LORD shall smite Egypt: he shall smite and heal it: and they shall return even to the LORD, and he shall be intreated of them, and shall heal them. In that day shall there be a highway out of Egypt to Assyria, and the Assyrian shall come into Egypt, and the Egyptian into Assyria, and the Egyptians shall serve with the Assyrians. In that day shall Israel be the third with Egypt and with Assyria, even a blessing in the midst of the land: whom the LORD of hosts shall bless, saying, blessed be Egypt my people, and Assyria the work of my hands, and Israel mine inheritance"* (Isa. 19.21-25).

8

Again, no specific reference is made to Jerusalem, but the fact that the Egyptians will in the future offer sacrifices and oblations and make a vow of submission to God makes it most likely that they will be among the worshippers in the temple.

So all nations will indeed **worship** at Jerusalem – the form of that worship not being specified – but here is the first, and we believe only, reference to a nation other than Israel actually **offering sacrifices.**

Ezekiel's testimony

Thus far we have looked at passages outside the prophecy of Ezekiel. But to establish the specific identity of the temple worshippers, and especially those who will offer sacrifices on its altar, we clearly need to go to his account of the temple. We find that the prophet is very specific about this when he outlines *"all the ordinances of the house of the LORD"* (Ezek. 44.5).

God first lists Israel's previous laxity: *"Ye have brought into my sanctuary strangers, uncircumcised in heart, and uncircumcised in flesh, to be in my sanctuary, to pollute it, even my house, when ye offer my bread, the fat and the blood, and they have broken my covenant because of all your abominations. And ye have not kept the charge of mine holy things: but ye have set keepers of my charge in my sanctuary for yourselves."* Having thus reproached them for their past failings, God then lays down the criteria for entry into His new temple: *"Thus saith the Lord GOD, no stranger, uncircumcised in heart, **nor uncircumcised in flesh**, shall enter into my sanctuary, of any stranger that is among the children of Israel"* (Ezek. 44.7–9).

There seems no escaping the meaning of these words: all who enter the new temple must be physically circumcised – having performed the act which formed the covenant between God and Israel. Israel are, by definition, "the circumcision", but should any strangers (the Hebrew word means "foreigners"), desire admittance, they must first be circumcised, even if they were actually dwelling among the Israelites. This, we suggest, would exclude the majority of world peoples, for there is no scriptural evidence that circumcision will be generally required in the Kingdom. But maybe the local nations, such as Egypt, who we have just seen will vow and sacrifice to God, will on this basis be permitted access to the future temple.

"A house of prayer for all people"

But what of that famous passage in Isaiah that seems to predict that all nations will offer sacrifices in God's house of prayer? A closer examination shows that this passage, too, imposes a similar criterion for entry. If, rather than taking this passage out of its context and quoting only one phrase of it, we take the whole quotation we find that it describes admission to the temple as being very selective. In fact it is not speaking of the world at large but, like Ezekiel, of foreigners who desire entry; and it imposes similar conditions: *"Also the sons of the stranger, that join themselves to the LORD, to serve him, and to love the name of the LORD, to be his servants, every one that keepeth the sabbath from polluting it, and* **taketh hold of my covenant***; even* **them** *will I bring to my holy mountain, and make them joyful in my house of prayer: their burnt offerings and their sacrifices shall be accepted upon mine altar; for mine house shall be called an house of prayer for all people"* (56.6–7).

So this passage does not have a universal application, as is so often assumed. Along with Ezekiel, Isaiah restricts temple entry to those of "all people" who take hold of God's covenant, presumably by circumcision.

This allusion to a *"house of prayer for all people"* is reminiscent of Solomon's prayer for foreigners at the dedication of the first temple: *"Moreover concerning a stranger, that is not of thy people Israel, but cometh out of a far country for thy name's sake; ... when he shall come and pray toward this house; hear thou in heaven thy dwelling place, and do according to all that the stranger calleth to thee for"* (1 Kings 8.41–43). Here the foreigner was invited to *"pray toward this house"* as well as actually entering its precincts, and maybe this is the relationship that will exist between the nations of the world and the future Jerusalem temple. Those who come up to Jerusalem will look towards the house – maybe from the new city to be built south of the temple, *Yahweh shammah* (Ezek. 48.35), which, interestingly enough, can be translated: "To Yahweh from this place" (see page 111).

A temple for Israel

Closer examination of the details in Ezekiel supports the above suggestions that Israel (together with any circumcised proselytes) will be the primary worshippers in the temple and those who offer sacrifices. Those who traverse the temple courts and keep the "solemn feasts" are the *"people of the land"* (46.3,9), as are those for whom sacrifices are offered (45.16,22). Those sacrifices *"make reconciliation for the **house of Israel**"* (43.10; 45.17). The priests are to teach *"my people"* (44.23), and for their sustenance are to eat *"every dedicated thing **in Israel**"* (v.29). Thus all the services and festivals of the temple seem to be directed to Israel. Will Israel's unique access to the temple and its ritual highlight the nation's future supremacy that is often described by the prophets?

But any foreigners who settle in the land, and presumably enter into God's covenant, can be given an inheritance along with Israel (47.22) and enter the temple.

Summary

In the opening chapter we said that our approach would be to let Scripture speak for itself, hoping that our readers would try to rid their minds of any preconceptions that would hinder an understanding of that message. In summary, the scriptural teaching that we have considered to date suggests that:

- A temple will yet be erected in Jerusalem, the city that will be the seat of Christ's administration of the Kingdom.

- The temple will be primarily a place of worship and sacrifice for Israel and for any foreigners who accept circumcision.

- All other nations will be invited to pray towards the temple.

- People from all other nations will be invited to visit Jerusalem and to worship there, but we could not find a reference that suggests that they will enter the temple to offer sacrifices.

- Those who take part in the latter-day attack on Jerusalem will be invited to Jerusalem to keep the Feast of Tabernacles.

- Egypt, possibly along with Assyria, will sacrifice to God and vow allegiance to Him.

If this is a correct understanding of the purpose and function of the future temple, it obviously has implications for the size of the building; and this is the topic for our next chapter.

Chapter 3 The question of size

In the previous chapter we suggested that the size of the future temple could be influenced by the numbers of those who will be actively engaged in its services. These will be primarily the nation of Israel and any who *"take hold"* of God's covenant (Isa. 56.6–7). We now consider the information supplied by Ezekiel and other prophets in an attempt to determine the overall dimensions of the new temple.

In common with the descriptions of the tabernacle constructed in the wilderness and the temple built by Solomon, the measurements of the future temple described by Ezekiel are given in great detail. It would be thought, therefore, that it should not be difficult to determine at least an outline plan of the proposed building, as is possible for the earlier structures. But over the years at least three different suggestions for the overall design have been advanced for the temple seen by Ezekiel.

The main reason for this is that whilst the majority of the measurements are clearly specified, some, especially a few crucial ones that relate to its size, are either not defined or are ambiguous. In an attempt to address this problem we are conscious of our limitations and the following expresses an understanding which is put forward as a suggestion.

The measuring tools

The man of symbol, who in vision conducted Ezekiel through the new temple, had two measuring implements – a *"line of flax"* (a *"builder's line"*, LXX) and a *"measuring reed"*, or *"rod"* (Ezek. 40.3). There is no record of the builder's line being used for delineating the dimensions of the temple itself; its first mention is in connection with the sequential measuring at thousand-cubit intervals of the deepening waters that came from the temple (47.3). This line was presumably used only for measuring lengthy distances.

The basic measurement was the cubit, usually taken as the distance from the elbow to the fingertips, about 45 cm or 18 inches (the word coming from the Latin *cubitum* or "elbow"). But in measuring the temple a larger cubit was used, the *"cubit and an handbreadth"* (40.5). The handbreadth was the distance across the palm at the lower end of the fingers, about 74 mm or 3 inches. This gives the total length of the temple cubit as 54 cm or 21 inches.

The measuring reed held by Ezekiel's guide was a rod with a total length of 6 of these larger cubits: about 3 metres or 10 feet. Presumably it was subdivided into cubits to enable smaller measurements to be taken.

Some uncertainty in translations

The vast majority of the temple measurements are in cubits, both in the original Hebrew and in any translation of it, but in some cases the unit of measurement is not specified in the original text. In these instances the translators have often made their own assumptions, based on the context, and inserted what they think was intended. In such cases the KJV and NKJV put these additions in italics, but the RSV and NIV insert the word "cubit" without any indication that the word for that unit of measurement does not occur in the original.

For example, in giving the dimensions of the temple altar, chapter 43.13 clearly specifies that the measurements are in cubits: *"And these are the measures of the altar after the cubits: The cubit is a cubit and an hand breadth."* But then, after giving precise details of some measurements, in the original the total length of the side of the altar is given simply as *"twelve long, twelve broad"* (v.16). In view of the statement of verse 13 it is presumably correct to insert "cubits" alongside the "twelve long" – which the KJV does in italics. But some translations add it in the normal typeface, from which the ordinary reader might assume that the word is in the original. Other expositors have used the ambiguity to claim that the altar is twelve reeds in length – giving a much larger total dimension.

Possibly the most important area of uncertainty is in the overall dimensions of the sanctuary. Ezekiel's guide measured the outer walls, each being *"five hundred reeds with the measuring reed"* (42.16–19 KJV). In this case the original for "reeds" is in the manuscripts on which the KJV is based. But the confusion is that virtually all other versions follow the Septuagint, which clearly has the word for "cubit" rather than that for "reed". It is also worth noting that in the KJV the units of the sanctuary's dimensions are not stated in Ezek. 45.2, but some "suburbs" are clearly measured in cubits, suggesting that these were intended throughout.

What, in practical terms, are the implications of using either reeds or cubits where the unit of measurement is not stated or is ambiguous?

Figure 1

Two alternative sizes for the holy oblation. The area occupied by a square of side 25,000 **reeds** that includes Jerusalem (L) compared with one of side 25,000 **cubits** (R).

Consider the holy oblation in which the sanctuary is sited (Ezek. 45.1–6). If its dimensions are taken as "reeds" (i.e. six cubits) it will be a square with each side about 81 km (50 miles) long. If in "cubits", the corresponding measurement will be about 12.5 km (8 miles). Or in the case of the sanctuary itself, the building will be about 1.5 km (1 mile) square if measured in reeds, or 270 metres (875 feet) square if in cubits (see Figure 1).

Taking the whole scriptural context

How does one decide which measurement is correct, or at least, the most likely? We suggest that we need to bring other Scriptures to bear on the situation, many of which define the geography and topography of the land in the future. For example, the holy oblation is a square of 25,000 units on each side. If those units are reeds it describes an area of 6500 or more km². As it must include Jerusalem, such an area would extend to the Mediterranean to the west and completely cover the northern part of the Dead Sea to the east. This latter area somehow does not seem appropriate for a sanctified portion; for here mundane occupations such as fishing will be carried out, and the banks of the sea contain salty marshes (47.10–11). Therefore, in this case it would seem that the assumption that the intended measurement is in cubits is more appropriate (see Figure 1).

The size of the sanctuary

The overall size of the actual temple complex is not so easily determined. Which is correct, the KJV "reeds" or the "cubits" of other versions based on the Septuagint? In an earlier chapter it was shown that the new temple will be sited at Jerusalem, and there are several other predictions relating to the time of the end that affect that city. For example, speaking of Jerusalem, God predicts through Jeremiah: *"Thus says the LORD: Behold, I will restore the fortunes of the tents of Jacob, and … **the city shall be***

rebuilt upon its mound, and the palace [Heb. *armown* from an unused root, meaning "to be elevated"] **shall stand where it used to be** … *In the latter days you will understand this"* (30.18–24, RSV). This seems to suggest that latter-day Jerusalem will largely follow its ancient boundaries, and its major building will be on the same site.

In the next chapter those future boundaries of Jerusalem are defined: *"Behold, the days come, saith the LORD, that the city shall be built to the LORD from the tower of Hananeel unto the gate of the corner. And the measuring line shall yet go forth over against it upon the hill Gareb, and shall compass about to Goath. And the whole valley of the dead bodies, and of the ashes, and all the fields unto the brook of Kidron, unto the corner of the horse gate toward the east, shall be holy unto the LORD; it shall not be plucked up, nor thrown down any more for ever"* (31.38–40). Whilst not all of these places can be located with certainty, they are certainly within the local environs of the ancient city. This seems to rule out a reconstruction that will be much larger than the city of Jeremiah's day.

Other references state that the future Jerusalem will have what one might term "ordinary" residents: *"Jerusalem … shall be lifted up, and inhabited in her place, from Benjamin's gate unto the place of the first gate, unto the corner gate, and from the tower of Hananeel unto the king's winepresses"* (Zech. 14.10); *"Thus saith the LORD; I am returned unto Zion, and will dwell in the midst of Jerusalem: and Jerusalem shall be called a city of truth; and the mountain of the LORD of hosts the holy mountain … There shall yet old men and old women dwell in the streets of Jerusalem, and every man with his staff in his hand for very age. And the streets of the city shall be full of boys and girls playing in the streets thereof"* (Zech. 8.3–5). And Jeremiah predicts that the streets of Jerusalem will hear, *"The voice of joy, and the voice of gladness, the voice of the bridegroom, and the voice of the bride, the voice of them that shall say, Praise the LORD of hosts … and of them that shall bring the sacrifice of praise into the house*

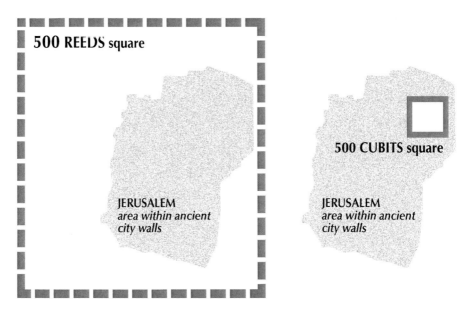

Figure 2 Two alternative sizes for the sanctuary. The area occupied by a square of side 500 reeds that includes Jerusalem (**L**) compared with one of side 500 cubits (**R**).

of the LORD" (33.11). Combining these three factors: Jerusalem to be rebuilt on its old site, having a mortal population and at the same time being the site of the temple, we are in a better position to suggest which of the two alternatives – reeds or cubits – applies to the overall size of the temple building.

Again, it is best to display the alternatives visually. Figure 2 shows the size of the two alternatives. It will be readily seen that the larger area would extend well beyond the old city boundaries, rendering difficult, if not impossible, the fulfilment of the above prophecies.

This, coupled with the pointers that those who partake in the actual temple rituals will be primarily Jews or proselytes as suggested in the last chapter, indicates that the smaller dimensions of Ezekiel's temple specifications would be more appropriate. In later chapters we hope to show that the detailed measurements which the prophet was given fit in exactly with this supposition.

As always in such considerations of prophecies yet to be fulfilled, it is impossible – not to say God-dishonouring – to be dogmatic as to details. We are very conscious of this and repeat that the foregoing is a personal view and only put forward as a suggestion.

Chapter 4 **The plan of the sanctuary**

Turning, now, to a more detailed look at the description of the future temple, we first note the main division of the last nine chapters of Ezekiel. There are three distinct sections:

● Chapters 40–42: The temple structure

● Chapter 43: God enters the building

● Chapters 44–48: The temple in operation

"The frame of a city"

When Ezekiel in vision saw the new temple from the vantage point of the *"very high mountain"* he described it as *"the frame of a city on the south"* (40.2). The word "frame" is not used elsewhere in Scripture, so one cannot use other passages to help understand its meaning. Other versions translate the phrase as *"something like the structure of a city"* (NKJV, RSV), and *"some buildings that looked like a city"* (NIV). It was clearly a substantial series of buildings.

The term *"frame of a city"* does not necessarily denote an extensive area in modern terms. If the smaller size of the sacred area is considered appropriate, it still represents a big city compared with many in Ezekiel's day. In modern measurements a square of 500 cubits each side occupies 7.13 hectares (17.6 acres), and this is larger than many cities in Ezekiel's day. The site of Megiddo extended over about 2.8 hectares (7 acres), that of Jericho 2.4 hectares (6 acres) and that of Shechem 4 hectares (10 acres).

General points

It may be as well at this stage to mention some features of the description that are of general application:

- To prevent confusion a distinction should be made between the terms "the sanctuary" and "the temple". In most cases "the sanctuary" refers to the whole complex of buildings and courtyards; and "the temple" or "house" (KJV) indicates the central building described in detail in chapters 40.48–41.26.

- Generally speaking, ground plans only are measured and described. There are only a few measurements that refer to the height of any structures.

- Compared with the descriptions of the tabernacle and Solomon's temple there is little reference to furniture, no mention being made of the ark, lampstand, table of shewbread and laver.

- An even more unexpected omission is any reference to gold, which was such an outstanding feature of the earlier sanctuaries; although no doubt the buildings will be imposing and beautiful: *"The glory of this latter house shall be greater than of the former, saith the LORD of hosts"* (Hag. 2.9).

Ezekiel's guide

Arriving at the building, Ezekiel was met by a man whose appearance was like *"shining brass"* (LXX) – possibly linking back to Ezekiel's opening vision of the cherubim (1.7) – who invited the prophet to see, hear and set his heart on all that he was about to be shown. This guide, presumably an angel, then took Ezekiel on a detailed tour of the buildings that made up the sanctuary. As mentioned previously, this guide had two measuring implements: a "reed" or rod 6 cubits (3 metres) long, and a flaxen line which presumably was used for measuring the longer distances.

We will now follow Ezekiel and his guide as they enter and survey the various features of the sanctuary. Rather than stop en route to examine every detail we will try, at first at least, to get a general picture of the layout. As mentioned previously, this will be based on a 500 cubit square sanctuary into which, we believe, the various dimensions measured by the angel fit simply and naturally. Often we will use the RSV translation, which helps in the understanding of the descriptions.

A wall with gateways

Approaching from the outside, the first thing encountered was a wall that entirely surrounded the square area. It was 3 metres (10 feet) high and of a similar thickness (Ezek. 40.5). On the eastern side was a *"gate"* which the pair then approached (v.6). From the description and measurements this was not a simple gate, but an imposing entrance or gateway, 60 cubits high (over 30 metres or 100 feet). Going up a stairway of seven steps (vv.6, 26) Ezekiel and his guide walked through the entrance of this gate and

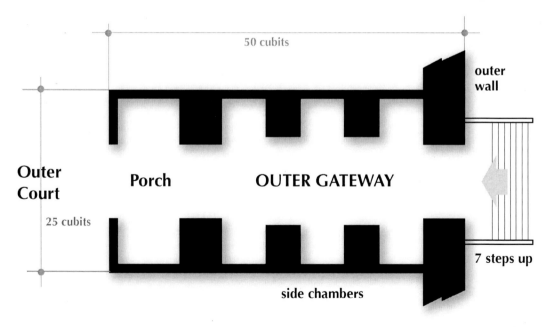

Figure 3 Plan showing part of outer wall with gateway.

saw and measured three small rooms on each side (v.10). At the far end was a *"porch"* (KJV) or *"vestibule"* (RSV). This is shown in Figure 3.

The overall dimensions of this gateway with its side rooms are then given. First the width: *"From the back of the one side room to the back of the other, a breadth of five and twenty cubits"* (v.13, RSV, as are most references in this chapter). So the total width of the gate structure was 25 cubits. The total length was then measured: *"From the front of the gate at the entrance to the end of the inner vestibule of the gate was fifty cubits"* (v.15).

We thus have the first feature that has been described – a gateway of dimensions 50 x 25 cubits. Only one gate is mentioned on this east side, and it is a reasonable assumption (confirmed by other features that we will find) that this single entrance is in the centre of the 500 cubit wall.

Identical gates were positioned on the north side (v.20) and the south side (v.24). It is very important to note that there was no west gateway mentioned – the reason for which will become apparent in our later studies. These three gates comprise the *"gates of the entrance"* or *"outer gates"* (v.15), as distinct from the *"inner gates"* that Ezekiel saw later.

The outer court and chambers

Going back to the description of the east gate: having described and measured it, the guide took Ezekiel through the rear of the gateway into what is described as the *"outer court"* (v.17). In this court was a *"pavement"* which *"ran along the side of the gates, corresponding to the length of the gates; this was the lower pavement"* (v.18). So we need to imagine the three gates jutting out into a courtyard, and alongside the gates, and level with their rear entrances, was a pavement, termed the *"lower pavement"*. Presumably somewhere else there was an upper pavement.

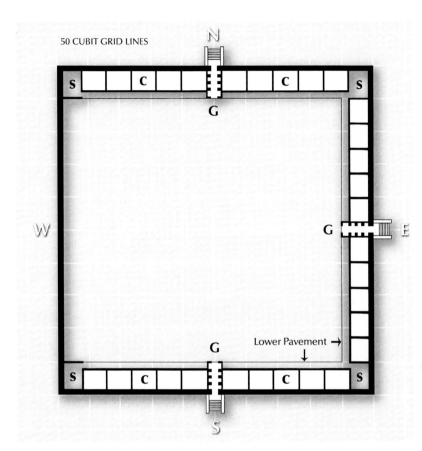

Figure 4

Plan of the outer court and chambers. The grid lines, at 50 cubits, are for measurements: they are not part of the plan.

G = the three gates

C = the 30 chambers on the pavement

S = the small corner courts

Sited on this pavement was a series of rooms, or *"chambers"*, thirty in all: *"Then he brought me into the outer court; and behold, there were chambers and a pavement, round about the court; thirty chambers fronted on the pavement"* (v.17). No size or arrangement of these chambers is mentioned, but it is reasonable to assume that there were ten on each side of the courtyard, five on either side of each gate.

Although Ezekiel was not immediately shown the structures at the corners of the outer court, for completeness we can note that there were areas in each corner: *"Then he brought me forth to the outer court, and led me to the four corners of the court; and in each corner of the court there was a court – in the four corners of the court were small courts, forty cubits long and thirty broad; the four were of the same size"* (46.21–22). We can now draw all these features – the gates, lower pavement, chambers and the corner courts – on a plan that we will gradually build up as this study proceeds. To help visualise the dimensions the grid lines are spaced at 50 cubits apart (see Figure 4).

The inner gateways

Having measured the east gateway, Ezekiel's guide then went from that gate into the outer court, and measured 100 cubits out from each of the three gateways. At this distance from each gateway was another gate that led to an *"inner court"*. Here are the references for each of the three gates, starting with the eastern outer gate: *"Then he measured the distance from the inner front of the lower gate to the outer front of the inner court, a hundred cubits"* (40.19); *"And opposite the gate on the north, as on the east, was a gate to the inner court; and he measured from gate to gate, a hundred cubits"* (v.23); *"And there was a gate on the south of the inner court; and he measured from gate to gate toward the south, a hundred cubits"* (v.27).

This seems quite straightforward. Ahead of each outer gate across the 100 cubit width of the outer court there was another gate, which led into an inner court. Each of these inner gates was similar in plan and size to the outer gates, that is, 50 x 25 cubits (vv.28–9,33,35). One difference was noted: whereas the outer court gates were approached by means of seven steps, the inner court gates had eight (v.31). So the ground level rose as one drew near the centre of the sanctuary.

Ezekiel and his guide then went through this inner gate into the inner court. It can be seen from Figure 5 (overleaf) that the central area inside the inner gates is a square, 100 cubits each way. This is confirmed by the

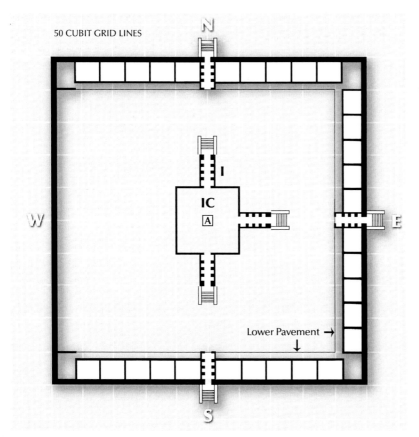

50 CUBIT GRID LINES

N

W

S

E

IC

A

I

Lower Pavement →

Figure 5

The three inner court gates (**I**) leading into the 100 x 100 cubit square inner court (**IC**), with the altar (**A**).

angel's later measurement: *"And he measured the court, a hundred cubits long, and a hundred cubits broad, foursquare"* (v.47). So the size of this inner court is quite definitely stated as 100 x 100 cubits.

The altar in front of the temple

But immediately after recording the size of this inner court, there comes a most enlightening statement: *"and the altar was in front of the temple"* (v.47). This tells us two things: (1) the altar was in the inner court, and (2) it was in front of the actual temple. As we will see shortly, Ezekiel's guide indicated that on the north, south and east sides of the inner court there were buildings for the priests' use. Thus the very strong inference is that the temple is on the west side of that court. If this is so, it can be readily seen why there was no gate on the west side of the sanctuary. And the presence of buildings for the priests and offerings in this vicinity suggests that the altar and the actual temple building are nearby.

The inner court buildings

Ezekiel gives more details of these arrangements. He was taken into the inner court, and on either side of the inner court gates, and surrounding the court on the three sides, he saw a series of buildings: *"Then he brought me from without into the inner court, and behold, there were two chambers in the inner court, one at the side of the north gate facing south, the other at the side of the south gate facing north"* (v.44). No specific dimensions of these buildings are given, but it can be inferred from the fact that they were *"at the side"* of the inner gates that they had the same width as the gate, that is, 50 cubits. The function of these "chambers" was then explained to Ezekiel: *"And he said to me, This chamber which faces south is for the priests who have charge of the temple, and the chamber which faces north is for the priests who have charge of the altar; these are the sons of Zadok, who alone among the sons of Levi may come near to the LORD to minister to him"* (vv.45–6) (see **a** and **b** in Figure 6 overleaf).

Adjacent to these was another chamber: *"There was a chamber with its door in the vestibule of the gate, where the burnt offering was to be washed"* (v.38) (see **c** in Figure 6).

Later in his tour Ezekiel was taken back to the outer court (KJV) or possibly the inner court (RSV) (**IC** in Figure 6 – in fact the side from which he was looking does not affect the description) and saw some more buildings: *"Then he led me out into the inner court, toward the north, and*

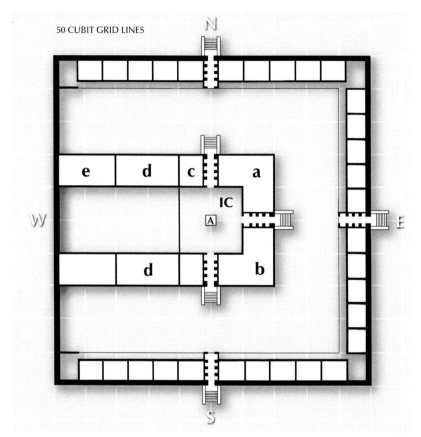

Figure 6

The inner court buildings.

For key to chambers see text.

he brought me to the chambers which were opposite the temple yard and opposite the building on the north. The length of the building which was on the north side was a hundred cubits, and the breadth fifty cubits" (42.1–2).

There was a similar building on the southern side. Of these, Ezekiel's guide said: *"The north chambers and the south chambers opposite the yard are the holy chambers, where the priests who approach the LORD shall eat the most holy offerings; there they shall put the most holy offerings … for the place is holy"* (v.13) (see **d** in Figure 6).

Alongside the western end of these chambers on the north (and possibly south) were places where the priests prepare the offerings for the altar: *"Then he brought me through the entrance, which was at the side of the gate, to the north row of the holy chambers for the priests; and there I saw a place at the extreme western end of them. And he said to me, 'This is the place where the priests shall boil the guilt offering and the sin offering, and where they shall bake the cereal offering, in order not to bring them out into the outer court and so communicate holiness to the people'"* (46.19–20). The dimensions of these areas are not given, but presumably they continued the 50 cubit width of the holy chambers alongside them (see **e** in Figure 6).

A neat fit

So far in this reconstruction it has been possible to follow the details given in Ezekiel's description without any need to give his words anything other than their straightforward meaning, with all the measurements fitting neatly into the available space. It is also possible to follow his itinerary as he was guided from one place to another in a logical sequence. This suggests that this approach is in harmony with the record, even if some of the details remain uncertain.

It will be seen from Figure 6 that the area remaining on the west side of the inner court is 200 x 100 cubits. This was the area to which Ezekiel was next taken, and the details of the buildings and courts that it contained will be the topic of the next chapter.

Chapter 5 **The temple area**

So far we have gradually assembled a possible layout of the buildings of the sanctuary from the information given to Ezekiel by his guide (see Figure 7). At the conclusion of the previous chapter we noted that to the west of the inner court, in which was sited the altar, there was an area of 200 x 100 cubits (shaded in Figure 7).

Ezekiel was next taken to describe the buildings in this space, as recorded in the last two verses of Ezekiel 40 and the whole of chapter 41.

Three components of this area are described: *"the house"* or *"temple"*, the *"separate place"* or *"temple yard"* (RSV) and *"the building"*.

The first of these structures to be visited was the temple itself: *"Then he brought me back to the door of the temple* [to]... *the threshold of the temple toward the east (for the temple faced east)"* (47.1, RSV, as are most of the following references in this chapter). The angel then measured the side of the temple: *"Then he measured the temple, a hundred cubits long"* (Ezek. 41.13), and later the eastern frontage, which included the separate place or yard: *"Also the breadth of the east front of the temple and the yard, a hundred cubits"* (v.14).

Next he measured the *"building"*, which was also associated with the *"yard"*; *"And the yard and the building with its walls, a hundred cubits long"* (v.13). Verse 12 gives the location of this *"building"*: *"The building ... was facing the temple yard on the west side"*. So here we have two structures separated by a *"separate place"* or *"yard"*, or *"courtyard"* (NIV).

Adding together the given dimensions of these we have exactly the area remaining to the west of the inner court, that is, 200 x 100 cubits.

The east-west dimensions are:

    The temple: 100 cubits

    The *"building"* and *"separate place"* or *"yard"*: 100 cubits

    TOTAL 200 cubits

The north-south dimensions are:

    The temple and *"separate place"* or *"yard"*:

    TOTAL 100 cubits

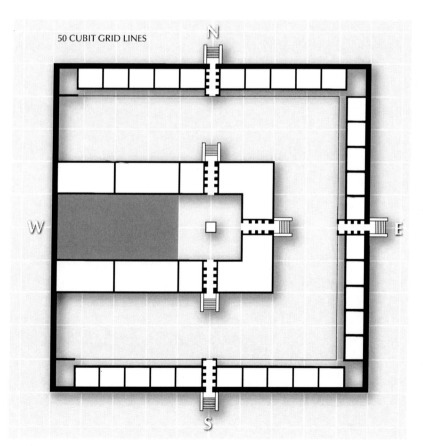

50 CUBIT GRID LINES

Figure 7

Shaded area shows the 200 x 100 cubit space to the west of the inner courtyard, described here as the "temple area".

31

The "building"

We must confess that prior to detailed studies of this topic we were not aware of this feature, which is clearly detailed. Its dimensions are given as follows: *"The building that was facing the temple yard on the west side was seventy cubits broad; and the wall of the building was five cubits thick round about, and its length ninety cubits"* (v.12). So here is a structure of internal dimensions 70 x 90 cubits, with a wall 5 cubits thick. This gives a total site area to the west of the temple complex of 80 x 100 cubits.

No other information is given about the *"building"*; we are only told its size, wall thickness and location. A wall of 5 cubits thick implies quite a substantial structure, and one of considerable height. No doors or any other access points are mentioned. More tantalisingly, we are not told its purpose. Will it be some sort of meeting place for those who by then will be able, as Jesus did in the past, to pass through solid barriers? Could it be the throne room of Christ? Who knows? We will have to wait and see.

But we can now see why there is no gateway on the western outside wall of the sanctuary; the *"building"* is there instead.

The separate place

This term, possibly more appropriate than the RSV *"yard"*, is alluded to earlier in this chapter, where we are given its dimensions: *"Between the platform of the temple and the chambers of the court was a breadth of twenty cubits round about the temple on every side"* (vv.9–10 RSV). Thus the separate place isolated the temple from its surrounding buildings by a space of 20 cubits. It would seem therefore (and this will be confirmed by the detailed measurements) that the temple itself was 60 cubits wide, and we have already noted that overall it was 100 cubits long.

This completes Ezekiel's description of the main areas of the sanctuary. Figure 8 shows the complete plan with all the areas shown in broad outline, including the three components just discussed, which fit exactly into the available space.

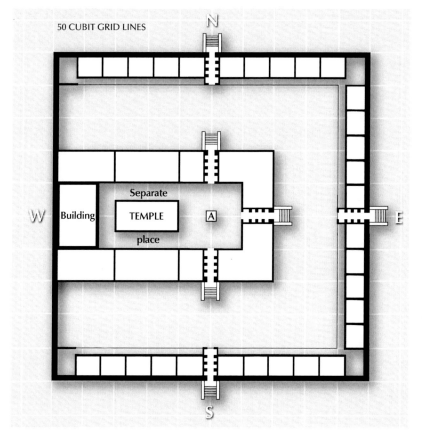

Figure 8

Showing:

the Temple
"the building"
"the separate place".

Chapter 6 **The temple in detail**

Having considered the general layout of the temple area we now look at the temple structure in detail. We will follow the route taken by Ezekiel and his guide as they left the inner court in which was the altar. As we have already seen, this altar was *"in front of the temple"*, and thus the temple itself faced east, that is, was on the west side of the inner court.

It will be helpful to refer to the numbered items in Figure 9 (plan) and Figure 10 (section) as the prophet's itinerary progresses. Not all the information given is readily understood and as we proceed we will have to make one or two small assumptions, but these will be seen to be justified when the complete plan is assessed.

The porch and steps

Ezekiel was then taken to the entrance to the temple, at which was a porch or vestibule with pillars on either side (**14** in Figure 9). The porch contained a flight of steps (ten according to the LXX) going up to the platform on which the temple was built. The dimensions of the porch were 20 cubits wide by 11 cubits deep. The RSV gives the height of this platform as 6 cubits: *"I saw also that the temple had a raised platform round about; the foundations of the side chambers measured a full reed of six long cubits"* (41.8). Thus, as progress was made through the sanctuary from the outside, there was a continual ascent: seven steps up to the level of the outer court, eight to the inner court, with a further flight up to the platform (Figure 10) on which the actual temple was sited.

The temple dimensions

Ezekiel's guide then took him into the temple, as described in chapter 41.1–11. They went through the entrance (**7** in Figure 9), of which we read:

"The breadth of the entrance was ten cubits; and the sidewalls of the entrance [**8** in Figure 9] *were five cubits on either side"* (41.2). The room that they entered measured 40 x 20 cubits: *"He measured the length of the nave forty cubits, and its breadth, twenty cubits"* (v.2). In view of the fact that the next chamber was called the *"most holy place"* (v.4), it is reasonable to assume that this first one was the equivalent of the holy place of the earlier temples (**9** in Figure 9): indeed it is of identical size (1 Kings 6.16–17).

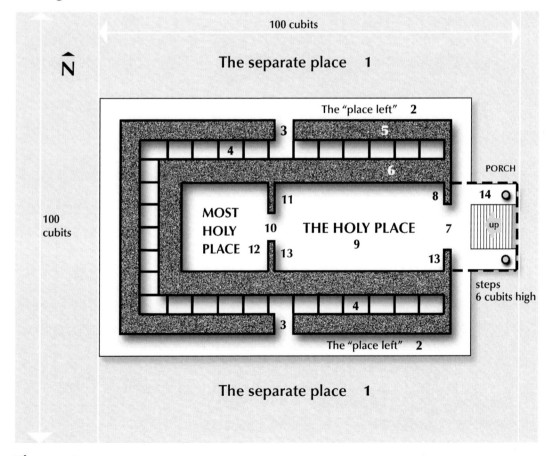

Figure 9   The temple plan in detail.

Then follows a significant comment that is often overlooked in studies of this topic. Having measured the holy place in the company of Ezekiel we are told that for the next measurement the angel went on alone: *"Then he went into the inner room"* (v.3). As we have seen, this room was the most holy place, a space that under the Law no ordinary mortal was allowed to enter, being a symbol of the time when God is manifested in flesh. It was therefore appropriate that Ezekiel was not then permitted to enter.

So the prophet watched from the adjoining room as the angel conducted the measurements of this most holy area. The doorway into it (**10** in Figure 9) was six cubits wide, with side walls of seven cubits each side (**11** in Figure 9). The thickness of this dividing wall (**13** in Figure 9) was two cubits (v.3, and one of the assumptions that we make is that this was also the thickness of the walls at the entrance into the holy place). The actual room (**12** in Figure 9) was 20 cubits square: *"And he measured the length of the room, twenty cubits, and its breadth, twenty cubits, beyond the nave. And he said to me, This is the most holy place"* (v.4). Again, this replicates the dimensions of the earlier temple (1 Kings 6.20).

Thus we can see from this reconstruction that the future temple is described as having a similar layout to that of the tabernacle and the temples of previous eras. As Peter says, the millennium will be a time of *"restitution of all things"* (Acts 3.21). The angel then measured the thickness of the temple wall, 6 cubits (**6** in Figure 9), and that of the surrounding side-chambers, 4 cubits (**4** in Figure 9) (v.5). These side chambers went all round the temple and, as in Solomon's temple, were in three storeys, with a stairway giving access to each. The size of the chambers progressively increased as one went from one storey to another. The outer wall of these chambers (**5** in Figure 9) was five cubits thick, beyond which was *"the place left"* (KJV) or *"the part of the platform that was left free"* (RSV) (**2** in Figure 9). This seems to be a sort of terrace that went all the way round the outer limits of the temple platform. It was

5 cubits wide (v.11) and the chambers were accessed from this terrace by doors on the north and south sides (**3** in Figure 9).

The separate place

We have already suggested that this was an open area (**1** in Figure 9) that went round the three sides of the temple, and this is confirmed by verses 9–10: *"Between the platform of the temple and the chambers of the court was a breadth of twenty cubits round about the temple on every side."*

Confirmatory measurements

As already noted, the overall dimensions of the temple are given as 100 x 100 cubits each way: *"Then he measured the temple, a hundred cubits long … also the breadth of the east front of the temple and the yard*

Figure 10 Diagram showing a possible vertical section of the temple area. The buildings of the inner court are separated from the temple by the *"separate place"* (**1**) in which the temple (**9**) is raised on a platform. The side walls of the temple contain chambers in three storeys, which are accessed from the *"place left"* (**2**), a terrace that surrounds the temple. No actual details are given of the height of the buildings, and none are intended to be conveyed in this section.

[separate place], *a hundred cubits"* (vv.13–14). Does the proposed layout with its dimensions add up to these overall specifications? Using the identification numbers on Figure 9 we can show that it does:

The length east to west		Cubits	Ref.
14	Porch	11	40.49
2	Place left (east side)	5	41.11
13	Thickness of door wall	2	41.3
9	Holy place	40	41.2
13	Thickness of door wall	2	41.3
12	Most holy place	20	41.4
6	Wall of temple (west side)	6	41.5
4	Side chambers (west side)	4	41.5
5	Side chamber walls	5	41.9
2	Place left (west side)	5	41.11
	Total	**100**	

The breadth north to south			
1	Separate place (N)	20	41.10
2	Place left (N)	5	41.11
5	Side chamber wall (N)	5	41.9
4	Side chambers (N)	4	41.5
6	Wall of temple (N)	6	41.5
9	Breadth of temple (N)	20	41.2,4
6	Wall of temple (S)	6	41.5
4	Side chambers (S)	4	41.5
5	Side chamber wall (S)	5	41.9
2	Place left (S)	5	41.11
1	Separate place (S)	20	41.10
	Total	**100**	

Chapter 7 **Further details of the temple area**

Having measured the temple area, Ezekiel's guide then showed him further features of the temple itself. Some of the details may not readily be envisaged, and from the variations in the various versions it seems that the original Hebrew is not always clear when translated. But there is no doubt as to the main aspects.

At the entrance to the temple was a double door, with a further double door shielding the entrance to the most holy place (KJV *"sanctuary"*): *"And the temple and the sanctuary had two doors. And the doors had two leaves apiece, two turning leaves; two leaves for the one door, and two leaves for the other door"* (Ezek. 41.23–24).

Inside, all the walls were panelled (KJV *"ceiled"*) with wood, on which was engraved a variety of figures. The original Hebrew for *"ceiled"* is unique to Scripture and its precise meaning is uncertain; but as lining with carved wood was a feature of the earlier temple (1 Kings 6.15–18) it is likely that wood panelling is also intended here. But unlike the previous temple there is no indication that this panelling was covered with gold.

Engraved figures

On every wall this wooden covering had figures carved on it: *"And it was made with cherubims and palm trees, so that a palm tree was between a cherub and a cherub; and every cherub had two faces; so that the face of a man was toward the palm tree on the one side, and the face of a young lion toward the palm tree on the other side: it was made through all the house round about"* (Ezek. 41.18–19).

Again this is very similar, but not identical, to the description of Solomon's temple: *"And he carved all the walls of the house round about* with carved figures of cherubims and palm trees and open flowers" (1 Kings 6.29). Ezekiel saw two of these earlier features, the palm trees and the cherubim, but he was given a more detailed description of these latter figures.

In common with the earlier temple, the cherubim and palm trees were also engraved on the doors of the temple and most holy place. Also, of the porch of the temple we read: "There were thick planks upon the face of the porch without" (Ezek. 41.25). Here the word translated "plank" is the usual one for "wood", and that translated "thick" is from a root that means "to cover". This may indicate that the internal panelling extended to the walls of the porch, or maybe, as the RSV suggests, it describes a wooden covering to the porch.

Palm trees

Palm trees are depicted in all areas of the future temple. They form the posts on either side of the gateway into the outer court (Ezek. 40.16, etc.) and to the inner court (v.34). As just noted, the temple itself had palm trees engraved on all the walls. They must therefore speak of a fundamental characteristic of those who desire to approach God.

What is the significance of these features, which are presented so uniformly in connection with the divine dwelling places? We can only make suggestions. The literal palm tree is conspicuous for its height and especially its straightness. These ideas are behind the Hebrew word for these trees: *tamar*, meaning "to be upright". Is this indicating that uprightness is the basic requirement in those who aspire to enter the divine presence? We would certainly gain this impression from the Psalms and Proverbs, where about two thirds of the word's scriptural usage is to be found. For example: "The righteous shall flourish like the palm tree" (Psa. 92.12), and especially: "Surely the righteous shall give thanks unto thy name: **the upright shall dwell in thy presence**" (Psa. 140.13).

The cherubim

The other impressive figures engraved on the temple walls were these symbolic objects, here seen with a significant variation (one assumes) from previous depictions. In the tabernacle and the first temple there is no indication that the cherubim had more than one face, but here two are described – that of a man and a young lion. From the fact that each face was looking at an intervening palm tree we assume that these heads were back to back.

In the next chapter we will take a detailed look at Ezekiel's first vision of the cherubim – this time with four faces – as recorded in chapter 1, and its reappearance on the occasion when God's glory entered the temple, as described in chapter 43. But at this stage we can say with some confidence that from their previous appearances in Scripture the cherubim are a symbol of the divine presence as manifested through other agencies. At present this is through the angels, but in the future it will be by the immortal saints. Thus the cherubim form a prominent feature of the most holy place in both tabernacle and temple, the compartment that symbolises the time when the faithful will enter *"within the veil"* (Heb. 6.19).

Why, then, in the future temple do the cherubim have two heads – of a man and a lion? And why in this case is a *young* lion specified, whereas the earlier buildings had mature ones? There is a special Hebrew word for "young lion", as distinct from the general term for "lion", and it almost exclusively denotes an immature beast. The places where "young lion" is used in Scripture almost always refer to its powerful activity. Micah speaks of a *"young lion among the flocks of sheep"* (5.8); and Isaiah of *"the young lion roaring on his prey"* (31.4). So does the young lion face of the cherubim symbolise the powerful activity of future spirit beings?

Another, more remote, association might be mentioned. The original word for "young lion" is *kefeer*, derived from the more familiar word *kaphar*, meaning "atonement", or "covering". As is well known, the original for "mercy seat", at which atonement was achieved, is *kapporeth*. So does the combination of a palm tree, human face and young lion symbolise those of the human race who, because of their uprightness, have had all their sins covered, and dwell in the presence of God?

The table before the LORD

Whilst inside the holy place Ezekiel describes an altar – the only piece of furniture mentioned as being in either the holy or most holy place. As often occurs, inserting punctuation into the unpunctuated original Hebrew text results in slightly different renderings, and this RSV version is based on the Septuagint: *"In front of the holy place was something resembling an altar of wood, three cubits high, two cubits long, and two cubits broad; its corners, its base, and its walls were of wood. He said to me, 'This is the table which is before the LORD'"* (Ezek. 41.21–22).

The purpose of this altar, or table (the two terms are virtually interchangeable, see Mal. 1.7), is not specified, but it seems likely that it occupies a similar position relative to the most holy place to the altar of incense in previous temples, that is, at the entrance to the most holy place. There is no mention of other items such as the lampstand and shewbread table. Does this suggest that in the future prayer and praise will remain a vital part of the believer's life when other aspects will have been superceded?

When later describing the ministry of the sons of Zadok, the only ones who will be allowed into the inner court and the temple, God says that as well as offering animal sacrifices on the altar in the court, these priests will: *"enter into my sanctuary, and they shall come near to my table, to minister unto me, and they shall keep my charge"* (44.16). The actual nature of that ministry *"before the LORD"* is not defined but, by analogy from the past, it will probably be the offering of incense.

The altar

This leads us on to consider the altar of sacrifice in the inner court, adjacent to the east-facing temple (47.1). The actual location within the court is not stated, but it is assumed to be placed centrally. Details of this altar are given in chapter 43.13–17. Again, although the details are uncertain the overall picture seems clear. The altar was 12 cubits square, resting on a plinth (KJV *"settle"*) of 14 cubits square. It was probably 12 cubits high, including the *"horns"*, and was accessed on the eastern side by what the KJV terms *"stairs"*. The original word simply implies a "going up" and, in view of the prohibition of Exodus 20.26, it was probably a ramp rather than steps.

The healing waters

As our attention is still within the inner court it would be convenient to mention another feature; although it may not become operational until later, after God's glory has entered. In chapter 47 Ezekiel is again taken to the east-facing doors of the temple, where a cascade of water issued from under the raised threshold: *"Afterward he brought me again unto the door of the house; and, behold, waters issued out from under the threshold of the house eastward: for the forefront of the house stood toward the east, and the waters came down from under from the right side of the house, at the south side of the altar"* (v.1).

These waters are also referred to in other Scriptures. Joel predicts that: *"a fountain shall come forth of the house of the LORD"* (3.18); and Zechariah looks forward to the day when: *"living waters shall go out from Jerusalem; half of them toward the former sea, and half of them toward the hinder sea: in summer and in winter shall it be"* (14.8).

When Ezekiel saw these waters in vision they presumably flowed alongside the projecting porch and out into the inner court, where they passed by the altar on its south side. Did they then flow out and cross the outer court as well, for Ezekiel next describes them as coming out under the outer east gate? The waters then flowed down to the Dead Sea, but our present interest is in their purpose in the sanctuary itself.

We have already commented on the fact that furniture such as the laver is not present in the future temple description, but we suggest that the water flowing across the courtyards will be the laver's equivalent. In the Mosaic system the water in the laver was a source of cleansing that all who entered the holy place were obliged to use, washing hands and feet (Exod. 30.17–21). We suggest that the flowing water across the inner court

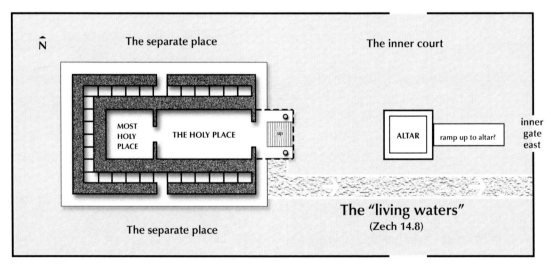

Figure 11 The east-facing temple in relation to the inner court and the altar of sacrifice. Ezekiel was shown water coming out from the south side of the threshold, presumably issuing from a point on the platform on which the temple was situated, and flowing through the court on the south side of the altar.

will have a similar purpose; the priests having to traverse this stream before entering the temple.

If, before the water finally emerges by the outer east gate (Ezek. 47.2), it flows across the outer court as well as the inner court, it will have to be crossed by the ordinary worshippers as they traverse between the north and south gates (Ezek. 46.9). Zechariah tells us that in the future: *"there shall be a fountain opened to the house of David and to the inhabitants of Jerusalem for sin and for uncleanness"* (13.1), and it is possible that washing in the flowing stream will be part of this process.

Chapter 8 **The glory of the LORD enters the sanctuary**

After showing Ezekiel the sanctuary's main features, his guide then took him to the eastern outer gate to witness the symbolic arrival of God into His house. The prophet saw the same vision of the divine glory that he had seen at the beginning of his ministry: *"It was according to the appearance of the vision which I saw, even according to the vision that I saw when I came to destroy the city: and the visions were like the vision that I saw by the river Chebar"* (Ezek. 43.3). On the previous occasion the glory of God had left the temple by the east gate (10.19; 11.22–23), and now it was returning through the same entrance.

It is therefore appropriate that at this juncture in our study we try to comprehend the significance of the visions of the glory of God, often termed "the cherubim", seen by this prophet.

The glory of God seen by Ezekiel is beyond our comprehension and powers of description. Even the inspired prophets could only use words to describe a manifestation that needed sight, sound and touch to be fully experienced – so our grasp of such a topic must inevitably be defective. The symbols are so unusual, almost bizarre, and so foreign to our world, that it might be felt that here is ground on which we cannot tread. Indeed, we cannot with any degree of certainty.

Yet these visions of cherubic glory are all part of God's revealed Word, given for our enlightenment; and although we cannot perceive all their implications, we can, and must, try to gain some overall understanding of the message they contain.

The cherubim

A survey of the scriptural references to the cherubim shows that they were symbols of how God has been "keeping", or preserving, *"the way of the tree of life"* (Gen. 3.24), by which way man can ultimately come to Him. This preservation frequently involved punishment of those who would corrupt that way, and so the cherubim are often revealed as fiery agents. It is suggested that in historical times these punitive agents were the angels.

Cherubim of judgement

So we come to the time of Ezekiel. There is no doubt that in the later times of the kings of Israel and Judah, God's way had been threatened. His people had turned out of His way, preferring instead the idolatrous practices of the surrounding nations. Thus they merited the fiery cherubic activity that resulted in the destruction of their country and especially their capital city, Jerusalem. It was this work of the cherubim in punishing Jerusalem that is depicted in those graphic symbols of Ezekiel chapter 1.

The symbols of Ezekiel's cherubim are relevant to this work. The *actual* agents of the destruction of Jerusalem were the Babylonians, coming down from the north, but the control of these events was under the hands of the angels in their cherubic activity.

Cherubim and the glory of the LORD

In chapter 1 Ezekiel saw coming from the north a fiery whirlwind, with unnatural brightness, out of which emerged four living creatures, associated with an extraordinary wheeled vehicle. Above this cherubic chariot, and presiding over the events, was the symbolic presence of God Himself. One can get so engrossed with the details in verses 4–25 that it is easy to pass over the focal point of the vision at the end of the chapter:

"And above the firmament that was over their heads was the likeness of a throne, as the appearance of a sapphire stone: and upon the likeness of the throne was the likeness as the appearance of a man above upon it ... This was the appearance of the likeness of the glory of the LORD" (vv. 26–28).

Thus the vision of the cherubim (in chapter 1 styled the *"living creatures"*) was subsidiary to this main revelation of the *"glory of the LORD"*. All the components of the earlier verses were the adjuncts to – and beneath – this primary concept: the *"likeness of a man"* on his throne – clearly a representation of God Himself, sitting supreme as Lord over all.

The part of the vision under the throne in a later chapter is termed *"the cherubim"* (Ezek. 10.15). There we are shown that these two parts of the vision – the *"cherubim"* and the *"glory of the LORD"* – can exist and function separately.

They originally appeared in unison: *"Then I looked, and, behold, in the firmament that was above the head of the cherubims there appeared over them ... as the appearance of the likeness of a throne"* (Ezek. 10.1). Later, the two separated: *"Then the glory of the LORD went up from the cherub..."* (v.4), only to be reunited later when the cherubic mission was accomplished: *"Then the glory of the LORD departed from off the threshold of the house, and stood over the cherubims ... And the cherubims lifted up their wings, and mounted up from the earth in my sight ... and the glory of the God of Israel was over them above"* (vv.18–19) (Note: the Hebrew suffix "im" indicates plurality, so the final "s" in the translation of "cherubim" is unnecessary).

So the overall picture is that of God – the likeness of a man on a throne – overseeing the cherubim and using them to carry out His will, whatever that may be at a given time. They are the vehicles by which God puts His intentions into practice.

Aspects of the cherubim

The various features of this vision symbolise the different facets of God's punishment of His people. Space forbids a detailed examination of all the symbols, but we will review the main aspects, leaving the details for individual study:

● *Fire*

The fire and the whirlwind clearly refer to impending judgement. Isaiah foretold: *"For, behold, the LORD will come with fire, and with his chariots like a whirlwind, to render his anger with fury, and his rebuke with flames of fire"* (Isa. 66.15). But as the vision unfolded, more features appeared.

● *Living creatures*

Out of the whirlwind and fire Ezekiel first saw four living creatures, with a predominately human appearance – *"they had the likeness of a man"* (Ezek. 1.5). But they also had specific non-human features: each had four wings, and each had four faces. Remember, these aren't literal beings; they do not exist as such anywhere (or at least, so we believe), but are figures, or symbols, of God's actions carried out by the angels.

● *Faces*

The four faces are described in verse 10. In the front, as the vision came towards Ezekiel, was a face of a man, on the right a lion, on the left an ox and in the rear an eagle.

First, a general comment on the symbolic use of "face". We often read of the face of God. He can make His face to either "shine" on people, that is, to bless them – or He can set His face "against" them to punish them. In this instance they are clearly coming for judgement on Israel.

What do we make of the four different faces? It is usually alleged that these stand for the four tribal emblems in the camp of Israel. This is clearly stated in rabbinical tradition and there is some, although not conclusive, scriptural evidence for this view. Thus it has often been assumed that the living creatures are symbolic of the nation of Israel. But this hardly fits in with the overall tenor of the vision, which is one of angels organising judgement on that unfaithful nation. As some have pointed out, the Israelite camp standards could have resulted from the symbol of the cherubim, rather than the other way round.

Do the differing faces speak of aspects of God's dominance over His creation? Do we here have man, wild animals (the chief being a lion), domestic animals (the largest and strongest being an ox) and the eagle (the greatest bird), all being subject to God's authority and, in keeping with the symbols, His judgement. It is interesting that Jesus, the manifestation of God to men, is described in four gospel records; the underlying aspects of each are generally reckoned to be described by these same four: man, lion, ox and eagle.

● *Wings*

Another notable feature was the wings. This obviously gives the idea of rapid movement, like an eagle to its prey. But there is probably more than just this. Ezekiel's cherubim shared this feature with the tabernacle cherubim, the seraphim of Isaiah and the living creatures of Revelation. Wings possibly speak of divine protection. The mercy seat was covered by the wings of the cherubim – an appropriate symbolic feature of those whose task is to *protect* God's way of life. Also the angels protect those who try to walk along God's way: *"In the shadow of thy wings will I make my refuge"* (Psa. 57.1). And Boaz refers to *"God ... under whose wings thou art come to trust"* (Ruth 2.12).

● *Feet*

The feet (v.7, better "legs") were "straight", like a human leg, not bent as in many animals. But the foot itself was like a calf's hoof, although bright and polished. Feet of calves and oxen were used to thresh out the corn – a process itself a symbol of divine judgement (e.g. Mic. 4.13). So here we have an apt symbol for the work these living creatures had to do.

● *Hands*

The cherubim had hands – a symbol of work: God's actions. These can be to punish or bless. God was either to *"stretch forth mine hand"* upon Egypt (Exod. 7.5); or He was to protect the faithful: *"According to the good hand of my God upon me"* (Neh. 2.8). So the hand is an appropriate symbol possessed by those carrying out God's work.

The chariot of the cherubim

Having described what we might call the riders in the chariot, Ezekiel considers the chariot itself. A notable feature is the wheels: *"Now as I beheld the living creatures, behold one wheel upon the earth by the living creatures … The appearance of the wheels and their work was like unto the colour of a beryl: and they four had one likeness: and their appearance and their work was as it were a wheel in the middle of a wheel. When they went, they went upon their four sides: and they turned not when they went"* (vv.15–17).

The original suggests that there was one wheel for each of the four living creatures – but they were not normal wheels, for there was *"a wheel in the middle of a wheel"*. Figure 12 shows what is possibly meant. The result was that they could go in any direction, but always in a straight line (they *"turned not"*). Thus they carried out the will of Him *"with whom there is no variation or shadow of turning"* (Jas 1.17). And the living creatures were never separated from the wheels (Ezek. 1.20–21).

The colour of the wheels was that of beryl, a precious stone. In the breastplate of the high priest, this stone represented the tribe of Dan, whose name means "judgement"; making it appropriate to the work of the cherubim.

The wheels were also *"full of eyes"*, as were the living creatures of Revelation, where eyes are called the *"seven spirits of God"* (5.6). So possibly the eyes refer to the all-seeing power of God, as manifested through the angels, to protect the faithful and to judge the wicked.

Figure 12 The wheels of the chariot

Brightness, heat and fire

And the whole aspect of this cherubic chariot was of brightness, heat and fire: *"As for the likeness of the living creatures, their appearance was like burning coals of fire, and like the appearance of lamps: it went up and down among the living creatures; and the fire was bright, and out of the fire went forth lightning"* (v.13).

Judgement on Jerusalem and the temple

Putting the vision of the cherubim in the context of Ezekiel 1, we can see that in symbol it represented angelic power coming to Jerusalem to execute God's judgements on the wicked city. Above the angels, and supervising their activity was the One on the throne, God Himself; He was also enveloped in fire.

Having seen the vision and been told of these impending judgements Ezekiel was commissioned to warn God's people (2.3-5). One of the cherubic hands gave him a scroll describing these judgements (2.9). No wonder (3.15) when he broached this message to the captives at Tel Abib, he sat there for seven days, astonished or "overwhelmed".

The predictions fulfilled

Thirteen months later Ezekiel saw the same vision, but this time it was not by the river Chebar, but had been transported in symbol to Jerusalem. The punishment was coming closer.

The same fire-wreathed being that had supervised the chariot of the cherubim appeared to the prophet and he was taken by the Spirit to Jerusalem, right into the *"inner gate* [of the temple] *which looketh toward the north"*, where the vision of the cherubim reappeared (8.1-4).

The rest of chapter 8 describes the defilement of God's house that necessitated these judgements, and then in chapter 9, the impending judgements are described. In chapter 10 the throne reappears over the cherubim, God giving a command to the one who in symbol is carrying out the punishments: *"Go in between the wheels, even under the cherub, and fill thine hand with coals of fire from between the cherubims, and scatter them over the city"* (v.2). This command was obeyed: *"He went in, and stood beside the wheels. And one cherub stretched forth his hand from between the cherubims unto the fire that was between the cherubims, and took thereof, and put it into the hands of him that was clothed with linen: who took it, and went out"* (vv.6-7). Here the cherubim are finally manifested in their punitive capacity – their fire was spread over the city.

To mark the final abandonment of the city, God in symbol gradually removed Himself. First, going up from the cherub (10.4), leaving the angels to continue the punishment of the city. Then He removed from the threshold back to the position above the cherubim (v.18). Next, the now united glory of the LORD and the cherubim went up from the earth to be over the east gate of the temple; and finally God departed to the Mount of Olives: *"Then did the cherubims lift up their wings, and the wheels beside them; and the glory of the God of Israel was over them above. And the glory of the LORD went up from the midst of the city, and stood upon the mountain which is on the east side of the city"* (vv.22–23).

In this way the cherubim and the associated glory of the LORD demonstrated in symbol God's impending judgements on the city, and then His removal from it. Jerusalem, and especially the temple, was no longer God's dwelling place.

The cherubim and glory return

But for Ezekiel this was not the end of God's message. As we are considering in this study, a future temple will be erected permanently in Jerusalem. And, again in vision, he saw this same glory of God returning – not this time for judgement, but for blessing.

But, we suggest, it will not be the angels who will then make up the symbolic cherubim. We read in Hebrews: *"Unto the angels hath he not put in subjection the world to come"* (2.5). Rather, as that passage goes on to say, the future control of the world – both to punish and to preserve – is in the hands of Christ and the redeemed. So the cherubim of the future are not the angels, but the multitudinous Christ; and it is these who are depicted in chapter 43 as returning to the future temple.

In this sense, God's glory will return by the way that it departed in Ezekiel's day. In the past the cherubim left by the east gate, and then from the Mount of Olives. They will come back using the same route in reverse. Zechariah, when speaking of the last days, says: *"And his feet shall stand in that day upon the mount of Olives, which is before*

Jerusalem on the east ... and the LORD my God shall come, and all the saints with thee" (14.4–5).

In Ezekiel chapter 43 the prophet sees the future reappearance of the manifestation of this cherubic glory: *"Afterward he brought me to the gate, even the gate that looketh toward the east: and, behold, the glory of the God of Israel came from the way of the east: and his voice was like a noise of many waters: and the earth shined with his glory. And it was according to the appearance of the vision which I saw, even according to the vision that I saw when I came to destroy the city: and the visions were like the vision that I saw by the river Chebar; and I fell upon my face"* (vv. 1–3).

Although it is the same vision of the cherubim and the glory of God that Ezekiel had seen previously, there appear to be subtle differences, which are appropriate to the new situation. There is no reference to a whirlwind, or to fire – this time the cherubim are not coming in judgement. Instead, the whole earth is filled with God's glory.

In this way Ezekiel foretells that God will finally and permanently return to dwell in His house, with all the previous defilement removed: *"And I heard him speaking unto me out of the house ... Son of man, the place of my throne, and the place of the soles of my feet, where I will dwell in the midst of the children of Israel for ever, and my holy name, shall the house of Israel no more defile"* (43.6–7).

What a wonderful comfort this must have been to Ezekiel, faced as he was with the imminent destruction of the temple he knew and loved. And what an incentive it is to those who are called to become components of the future cherubim. Their role then will be similar to that of the angels now – to judge an evil and disobedient world, and at the same time to extend divine mercy and protection to those in the millennium who will be walking along the way to the tree of life, as they once were.

Chapter 9 The ministers in the temple

At the beginning of chapter 4 we noted the threefold division of prophecy of the future temple. We have considered the first two of these: the temple structure, and the future entry of God into the building. We now examine the temple in operation (Ezek. 44.9–48.35). First, we consider those who officiate in the building.

Priests and Levites

Speaking of the time when Zion shall be called, *"The city of righteousness, the faithful city"*, God says: *"I will restore thy judges as at the first, and thy counsellors as at the beginning"* (Isa. 1.26). As one of the priestly functions is to judge and teach (Mal. 2.7), this suggests that in the future the old Levitical system will be reinstated. These ministers are described in Ezekiel either as "Levites" or the "sons of Zadok". So, as a basis for understanding the future roles it will help if we remind ourselves of the respective duties of these two groups under the Law of Moses.

The tasks of the Levites were clearly explained to Aaron: *"They shall keep thy charge, and the charge of all the tabernacle: only they shall not come nigh the vessels of the sanctuary and the altar, that neither they, nor ye also, die ... they shall ... keep the charge of the tabernacle of the congregation ... to do the service of the tabernacle of the congregation"* (Num. 18.3–4,6). Thus the Levites, although forbidden to serve as priests, were responsible for the manual tasks of caring for the tabernacle and, later, the temple structure, its day-to-day functioning and the all-important duty of singing praise to God.

Sadly, there developed a certain laxity in their service, as illustrated in the incident of Micah and the Danites (Judg. 17–18), and in their toleration of the idolatry that crept into the nation. But Malachi predicts that when the *"messenger of the covenant"* returns he will *"purify the sons of Levi, and purge them as gold and silver"* (3.1,3).

Thus reinstated, the Levites will be permitted to serve in the future temple in a very similar role as in the past. Indeed, Ezekiel uses almost identical language to that in Numbers: *"They shall not come near unto me, to do the office of a priest unto me, nor to come near to any of my holy things, in the most holy place: but they shall bear their shame, and their abominations which they have committed. But I will make them keepers of the charge of the house, for all the service thereof, and for all that shall be done therein"* (44.13–14).

The Aaronic priests

Whilst all those descended from Levi are termed "Levites", only those in the line of Aaron could minister as priests and be *"partakers of the altar"* (1 Cor. 10.18). God told Aaron: *"Thou and thy sons with thee shall keep your priest's office for every thing of the altar, and within the vail; and ye shall serve: I have given your priest's office unto you as a service of gift: and the stranger that cometh nigh shall be put to death"* (Num. 18.7). Thus, only the priests could offer the altar offerings and enter the actual tabernacle or temple in service to God.

But the priests had not only to offer the sacrifices on behalf of the congregation: a vital aspect of their ministry was that they were to eat some of the offerings. Leviticus records: *"This is the law of the sin offering: In the place where the burnt offering is killed shall the sin offering be killed before the LORD: it is most holy. The priest that offereth it for sin shall eat it: in the holy place shall it be eaten, in the court of the tabernacle of the congregation"* (6.25–26).

This eating of the offering was an indispensable aspect of the priest's service that had a vital bearing on his office. When, after the death of

Nadab and Abihu, *"Moses diligently sought the goat of the sin offering, and, behold, it was burnt: and he was angry with Eleazar and Ithamar, the sons of Aaron which were left alive, saying, Wherefore have ye not eaten the sin offering in the holy place, seeing it is most holy, and God hath given it you to bear the iniquity of the congregation, to make atonement for them before the LORD?"* (Lev. 10.16–17). Here was an important principle: when eating the sin offering the priest *"bore the iniquity"* of the offerer. This was pointing forward to the one who would share our nature and bear our sins, and so failure to eat would invalidate the type.

The priestly line from Aaron

Of Aaron's two sons, Eleazar succeeded him as high priest. His son, Phinehas, because of his faithfulness in the matter of Baal-Peor, when Israel "bowed down" to Moab's gods, was given a covenant of *"everlasting priesthood"*. God's words looked far into the future and have not yet been fully fulfilled: *"Phinehas, the son of Eleazar, the son of Aaron the priest, hath turned my wrath away from the children of Israel, while he was zealous for my sake ... Behold, I give unto him my covenant of peace: and he shall have it, and his seed after him, even the covenant of an everlasting priesthood; because he was zealous for his God, and made an atonement for the children of Israel"* (Num. 25.11–13).

But for a time the high priesthood temporarily transferred to the line of Aaron's other son, Ithamar (see 1 Sam. 14.3 (margin) and 1 Chron. 24.1–3). Eli, the high priest in the time of the judges, disgraced this other priestly line by failing to correct the excesses of his two sons or to prevent the loss of the ark of the covenant. As a result God predicted the end of the line from Ithamar and Eli: *"Behold, the days come, that I will cut off thine arm, and the arm of thy father's house ... And I will raise me up a faithful priest ... and I will build him a sure house; and he shall walk before mine anointed for ever"* (1 Sam. 2.31,35).

So the line through Ithamar and Eli was to terminate, reverting to the line of Eleazar and Phinehas, which, in a repetition of God's previous promise to Phinehas, would then become a *"sure house"* with a *"faithful priest"* who in the future would *"for ever"* walk before God's anointed.

The original "sons of Zadok"

This transfer back to the previous line happened in the days of David and Solomon. At this time the descendant of Eli was Abiathar who, it seems, ministered jointly with Zadok, who was descended from Phinehas. But in the time of David, Zadok had the pre-eminence, being always mentioned first (see 2 Sam. 20.25, etc.). In the attempted usurpation at the end of David's life, Abiathar joined the conspiracy for Adonijah; again showing the unfaithfulness of that line. As a result, in direct fulfilment of God's promise to Eli, Abiathar was expelled from the priesthood by Solomon: *"So Solomon thrust out Abiathar from being priest unto the LORD; that he might fulfil the word of the LORD, which he spake concerning the house of Eli in Shiloh"* (1 Kings 2.27).

From then on the high priesthood was in the hands of the sons of Zadok, that is, of the Aaronic line through Phinehas, which, God said, would have an *"everlasting priesthood"*. It seems that from that time this priestly line was known as the *"house of Zadok"*. For example, in the days of King Hezekiah we read of *"Azariah the chief priest of the house of Zadok"* (2 Chron. 31.10). Although no doubt these sons of Zadok did not consistently render acceptable service to God, their history is marked by notable occasions when they did uphold the true worship in the face of the false. We have already cited the case of Phinehas; in later times the fidelity of Zadok in support of David was followed by Jehoiada's removal of Baal worship from Judah in the days of Athaliah.

The Levitical priesthood will continue

Coming forward to the times in which Ezekiel prophesied, God promised through Jeremiah that as certainly as day follows night the throne of David would be re-established, and the Levitical priests would be there to offer sacrifices: *"For thus saith the LORD; David shall never want a man to sit upon the throne of the house of Israel; neither shall the priests the Levites want a man before me to offer burnt offerings, and to kindle meat offerings, and to do sacrifice continually … Thus saith the LORD; If ye can break my covenant of the day, and my covenant of the night, and that there should not be day and night in their season; then may also my covenant be broken with David my servant, that he should not have a son to reign upon his throne; and with the Levites the priests, my ministers"* (Jer. 33.17–21). The promise is clear: in the future the Levitical priestly role will persist, including their offering of sacrifices.

This is similar to God's words to Israel through Isaiah concerning the returned Jewish exiles: *"I will also take of them for priests and for Levites"* (Isa. 66.21).

Future sons of Zadok

So when we come to Ezekiel's reference to the priestly function in the future temple being exercised by the sons of Zadok, it would be reasonable, if not obligatory, to assume that they do so in fulfilment of God's promises of an everlasting priesthood mentioned to Phinehas, Eli, Jeremiah and Isaiah. It is the sons of Zadok who are to offer *"burnt offerings, and to kindle meat offerings, and to do sacrifice continually"*. Thus the literal descendants of Zadok (unknown to us but known to God) will fulfil the divine promise of an everlasting priesthood being continued to *"the Levites the priests, my ministers"*. If these priests are not the actual descendants of Zadok these repeated promises would be falsified.

The priests in the temple

With this essential background we can assess the references to the priestly functions in the future temple, which are contained in Ezekiel 44.15–31. First, the overall duties: *"The priests the Levites, the sons of Zadok, that kept the charge of my sanctuary when the children of Israel went astray from me, they shall come near to me to minister unto me, and they shall stand before me to offer unto me the fat and the blood, saith the Lord GOD: they shall enter into my sanctuary, and they shall come near to my table, to minister unto me, and they shall keep my charge … they minister in the gates of the inner court, and within"* (44.15–17). (Note: from what has already been adduced, the contention that vv.15–16 are parenthetical and refer to immortal priests is very difficult to sustain.)

Here Ezekiel outlines duties identical to the Mosaic offices – offering at the altar, coming near to God's table "within" the temple (v.17). And in common with the Mosaic priests, *"they shall eat the meat offering, and the sin offering, and the trespass offering; and every dedicated thing in Israel shall be theirs"* (v.29). But it would not be appropriate for immortal beings to eat the sacrifices and thus "bear the iniquity" of those offering them, because it is an established principle that the nature of the offerer and the atoning priest must be the same. Nor would the prohibition of wearing clothing that causes sweat when ministering in the inner court and "within" (i.e. in the temple, vv.17–18) be appropriate to immortal beings. The priests, the sons of Zadok, will continue the duty of judging and teaching; and all the other restrictions relating to clothing, diet, marriage and defilement that previously applied will continue, even with the possibility of their having to offer a sin offering (vv.18–31).

Thus the future temple will be serviced by the same two classes of ministers as under the Law of Moses: **(a)** the "ordinary" Levites being responsible for the outer areas of the structure, and also (again as in the past) for the praise of God that will be an essential feature of the

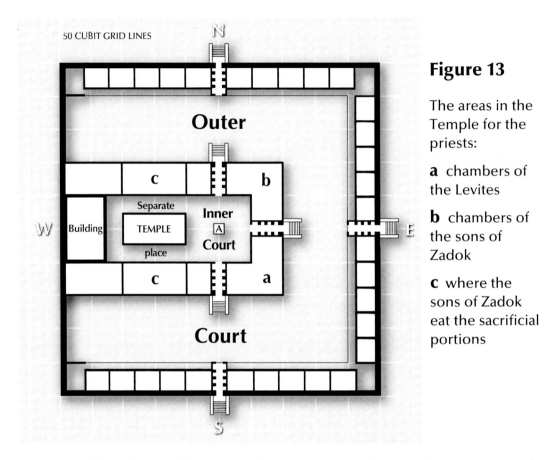

Figure 13

The areas in the Temple for the priests:

a chambers of the Levites

b chambers of the sons of Zadok

c where the sons of Zadok eat the sacrificial portions

sanctuary, but they will be denied access to the altar or the inner temple building; and **(b)** the Levitical priests, the sons of Zadok, offering and partaking of the altar sacrifices and entering the inner temple to minister at the *"table before the LORD"* (44.13,16).

Their respective areas of responsibility and the buildings they occupy are indicated in Figure 13 on the basis of the reference in chapter 40.44-46: *"And without the inner gate were the chambers of the singers in the inner court, which was at the side of the north gate; and their prospect was*

toward the south: one at the side of the east gate having the prospect
toward the north. And he said unto me, This chamber, whose prospect is
toward the south, is for the priests, the keepers of the charge of the
house. And the chamber whose prospect is toward the north is for the
priests, the keepers of the charge of the altar: these are the sons of Zadok
among the sons of Levi, which come near to the LORD to minister unto
him". It can be seen that being located adjacent to the inner court (**c** in
Figure 13) the priests will be able to fulfil the instruction not to go into
the outer court still wearing their holy garments (42.13–14; 44.19).

Kings and priests

In view of this suggested picture of the future, it might be asked: in what
sense will the redeemed immortal ones of the future occupy a priestly
office? For we are told that they will sing that Christ has *"made us unto*
our God kings and priests: and we shall reign on the earth" (Rev. 5.10). If
the foregoing is correct, then clearly the immortal saints will not be
priests who offer and eat of the altar sacrifices in the future temple. Also,
if the view that Ezekiel's priests are the redeemed is maintained, it would
be legitimate to ask why their reconciling ministrations are only
mentioned as being for Israel (45.17).

Zechariah foretold that in the future Christ would combine the roles of
priest and king, being a *"priest upon his throne"* (6.13), and it is
interesting that each time the saints are described as priests, a similar
dual function of king-priest is mentioned (Rev. 1.6; 5.10; 20.6). In this
capacity they will rule over the nations and, we suggest, fulfil the priestly
duties of teaching them, being the *"messenger of the LORD of*
hosts" (Mal. 2.7), and the interface between the subject peoples of the
Kingdom and Christ and his Father.

Chapter 10 **The prince**

Continuing our study of the ministers who service the future temple, we come to the one styled the "prince". As in all this study our objective is to let Scripture speak for itself.

"Prince" in scriptural usage

There are three Hebrew words most frequently translated as "prince": *nasi, nagid* and *sar,* all of which have the meaning of "prince", "captain", "chief", "ruler", "governor", etc., and are translated in Scripture by these various titles. The word used in connection with Ezekiel's temple is *nasi* (*Strong's* 05387), which has the basic meaning of something or someone that is lifted up, as is a ruler over those he rules. It does not of itself have the modern meaning of someone of royal descent. For example, the "princes" (Josh. 9.15, KJV) of the tribes of Israel are simply their "leaders" (NIV).

The *nasi* in Ezekiel's temple is translated as "prince" in all the versions that we have consulted, the translators clearly envisaging that a notable personage is here described. But in the original there is in fact nothing to indicate a difference from its customary meanings and usage as listed above.

Three main areas of activity are described for this prince, which we summarise below before examining them in more detail. Such a survey will help us suggest the nature and role of this important individual.

The prince and the sanctuary:

- Sits in, but does not pass through, the outer east gate.
- Enters and stands by the posts of the inner east gate.

The prince and sacrifices:

- Provides and prepares all the festive and regular sacrificial offerings.
- Prepares for himself and all the people the Passover and other tabernacle offerings, which are then offered on his behalf by the priests.

The prince's territory:

- He is given land on either side of the holy oblation, with the possibility of giving part to his sons and servants.

The prince and the sanctuary

Several activities are depicted for the prince in relation to the temple complex (see Figure 14 overleaf):

a sits in the outer east gate

Ezekiel was told that the outer east gate is to be permanently closed because (as we considered in a previous chapter) Yahweh had entered through it. In the original description of the gate (40.6–15) there is no mention of any method of closing the gateway so we cannot know the precise method of preventing ingress by this route. But on the inner face of the gateway, that is, on the end that opened out into the outer court, there was a porch (RSV "vestibule", NIV "portico") through which access could be gained to the gateway from the inside only. In effect this turns it into a room rather than an entrance way.

In this closed-off eastern outer gate the prince is to sit and engage in a sacred meal: *"It is for the prince; the prince, he shall sit in it to eat bread before the LORD; he shall enter by the way of the porch of that gate, and shall go out by the way of the same"* (Ezek. 44.3). Notice that the prince enters this area from the court; he does not proceed to the outside through the closed outer opening, but returns by the way that he went in.

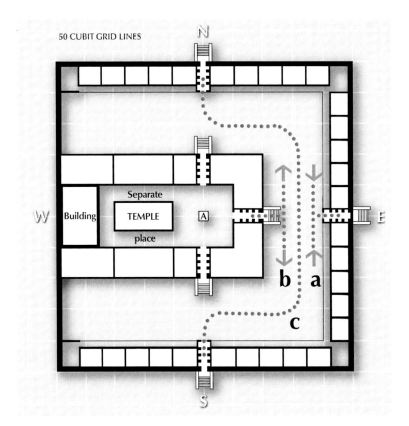

Figure 14:

The prince's movements:

a: into the blocked outer east gateway

b: into the threshold of the inner gateway

c: accompanying the mortal worshippers

So presumably he enters the sanctuary by the north or south gates, as do all the worshippers. He cannot enter through the closed east gateway.

b stands in the inner east gate

A similar stipulation applies to the inner east gate in connection with the offering of sacrifices in the inner court – the prince enters from the outer court and returns the same way: *"And when the prince shall enter* [the inner east gate], *he shall go in by the way of the porch of that gate, and he shall go forth by the way thereof"* (46.8). There is no reference to the prince actually entering the inner court, only an allusion to his standing at the gatepost (v.2). Whether this is the gatepost adjacent to the outer court or the one opening on to the inner court we are not told.

C conducts visiting worshippers round the outer court

When describing the passage of the mortal worshippers either northwards or southwards through the outer court *"in the solemn feasts"*, we are told that the prince accompanies them: *"And the prince in the midst of them, when they go in, shall go in; and when they go forth, shall go forth"* (46.9–10).

The prince and sacrifices

One of the major activities of the prince is to donate and prepare the sacrifices that will be offered by the sons of Zadok on the altar in the inner court on the occasions of the sabbaths, the new moons and the various feasts: *"And it shall be the prince's part to give burnt offerings, and meat offerings, and drink offerings, in the feasts, and in the new moons, and in the sabbaths, in all solemnities of the house of Israel: he shall prepare the sin offering, and the meat offering, and the burnt offering, and the peace offerings, to make reconciliation for the house of Israel"* (45.17). Note that he donates the sacrifice, rather than offering it on the altar.

All these offerings are initially to be assembled by the people and then placed in the hands of the prince, seemingly as a common stock of animals for use in the prescribed offerings: *"All the people of the land shall give this oblation for the prince in Israel"* (v.16). In this the prince has a similar role as, for example, Ezra, who gathered together animals for offering in the temple of his day (Ezra 7.16–17).

A specific mention is made of the Passover, when we are told that the prince is personally involved with the sacrifice: *"And upon that day shall* the prince prepare for himself and for all the people of the land a bullock for a sin offering" (Ezek. 45.22).

On the sabbath and the new moons there will be special arrangements, centred on the inner east gate. This gateway will normally be shut, and only opened on these particular occasions. The prince has a special function here: providing the offerings and handing them over to the priests for sacrifice in the inner court: "And the prince shall enter by the way of the porch of that gate without, and shall stand by the post of the gate, and the priests shall prepare his burnt offering [six lambs without blemish, and a ram without blemish, 46.4] and his peace offerings" (v.2).

Whilst these are being offered, the prince along with the people will: "worship at the threshold of the gate: then he shall go forth; but the gate shall not be shut until the evening" (v.2). Similar regulations will apply at the new moons (vv.6–8).

If, apart from these obligatory offerings, the prince desires to make a voluntary burnt offering the gate will be specially opened: "Now when the prince shall prepare a voluntary burnt offering or peace offerings voluntarily unto the LORD, one shall then open him the gate that looketh toward the east, and he shall prepare his burnt offering and his peace offerings, as he did on the sabbath day: then he shall go forth; and after his going forth one shall shut the gate" (v.12).

The prince's territory

As well as officiating in the sanctuary the prince will be given territory on either side of the holy oblation: "And a portion shall be for the prince on the one side and on the other side of the oblation of the holy portion, and of the possession of the city, before the oblation of the holy portion, and before the possession of the city, from the west side westward, and from *the east side eastward: and the length shall be over against one of the portions, from the west border unto the east border"* (45.7).

The prince will be able to pass on this inheritance to his sons for their permanent possession; but if gifted to his servants it will only be until the year of liberty: *"Thus saith the Lord GOD; If the prince give a gift unto any of his sons, the inheritance thereof shall be his sons'; it shall be their possession by inheritance. But if he give a gift of his inheritance to one of his servants, then it shall be his to the year of liberty; after it shall return to the prince: but his inheritance shall be his sons' for them"* (46.16–17).

The prince shall not wrongfully expel Israelites from their possession (e.g. as Ahab did to Naboth) or oppress the people in any way: *"Moreover the prince shall not take of the people's inheritance by oppression, to thrust them out of their possession; but he shall give his sons inheritance out of his own possession: that my people be not scattered every man from his possession"* (v.18).

Who is the prince?

Along with possibly the majority of my generation we were brought up to believe that the prince was Jesus, who will have returned to the earth immortal and glorious by the time this vision is fulfilled. But with further years of study it has become impossible to reconcile this with what seems to be clear teaching of Scripture – which obviously must come before any preconceived views. The difficulties are many, and will only be briefly touched on here in the form of questions for which answers should be given:

- As Jesus will be the embodiment of Yahweh, why would he be prevented from entering through the outer east gate because Yahweh had previously entered it?

- Would it be appropriate for the immortal Jesus there to "eat bread"; presumably to partake of the cereal offerings as did the priests of old (Lev. 2.3)?

- Why would Jesus have to stand at "the threshold" of the gateway to the inner court whilst a priest offers a sacrifice on behalf of himself and the people? If that priest is a mortal (see previous chapter) the difficulty is compounded.

- Why would Jesus feel the need to make a voluntary burnt offering for himself?

- Why is the prince not described as entering the inner court or the actual temple building?

- Would it be appropriate for the immortal Jesus at the Passover to prepare and offer a bullock "for himself" as well as the people of the land? He has already fulfilled all the types contained in the Passover.

- Is the prince described as having any priestly function?

- Would it not be demeaning for the King of kings and Lord of lords to act as an usher to the mortal temple visitors?

- Is it conceivable that Jesus would need the stipulation not to oppress or disinherit the people of the land?

- Why is there the inference that the prince does not have a permanent territorial inheritance but can pass it on to his sons?

What alternatives?

It has to be admitted that it is easier to see the problems relating to the identity of the prince than to make constructive suggestions as to who he will be. Jesus is undoubtedly "Messiah the Prince" (*nasi*) of Daniel 9.25 but, as noted above, the word is a general one for a ruler, so the link with Ezekiel's "prince" is not definitely established. The reference to David in

Ezekiel 37.25 saying that *"My servant David shall be their prince for ever"* presents similar problems: particularly that of an immortal being offering sacrifices. Also "David" is often taken in a representative sense as referring to David's greater Son, who will indeed be Israel's prince or ruler over the regathered tribes.

Undoubtedly the prince will be a person of immense standing and influence in the new temple, in fact the controller and overseer of all its activities. In times past the original temple had such a person, termed in Jeremiah 20.1 *"the chief governor* [nagid, also often translated "prince"] *in the house of the LORD"*. He was responsible to the high priest for the oversight of all the affairs of the temple. Could it be that such an office will be reinstated in the future, with one of the priests becoming this "prince" or "governor" responsible to Jesus for all the temple services? In this sense he would be Christ's representative in this new order.

Such considerations make us realise how imperfect is our knowledge and understanding of these divine things. None of us has the ability to make any authoritative pronouncement, far less to be dogmatic. It truly is the *"glory of God to conceal a thing"*. Meanwhile we look forward in faith to the time when in God's mercy and through the offices of our Saviour we shall *"know as we have been known"*.

Chapter 11 **The sacrificial ritual**

The ritual in the future temple seems to be mainly centred on the sacrifices offered on the altar in the inner court. In this it continues the emphasis on such offerings under the Mosaic dispensation. But although there are many similarities with the old system, in the future there will also be differences, which we believe must be significant, and for which we will make suggestions as we proceed.

The need for sacrifice

Some have difficulty with the concept of sacrifices in the future, not seeing the need for them because the redemption that the Mosaic ones foreshadowed has now been attained by the sacrifice of the Lamb of God. But it is generally accepted that the future offerings will call to remembrance the sacrifice of Jesus, in a similar way that the memorial breaking of bread service does for Christians today. It is a striking fact that in the book of Revelation the almost universal title for the returned Jesus is "the Lamb"; and this is true even when describing Jesus as King of kings and Lord of lords. We suggest that this title is used because even in the millennium the sacrifice of our Lord that has achieved such an outcome will always need to be remembered. The future sacrifices in the temple will be a means of ensuring this.

But for Israel there may be a more specific reason, which we will suggest later.

The Mosaic ritual

As the timetable of the future offerings will be based on the Mosaic ritual and calendar, with its typical significance, it is necessary to take these as the foundation on which to base our understanding of the future ritual.

Under the Law of Moses the religious calendar was based mainly on natural cycles: such as the day, the month, and the agricultural round of sowing and harvesting. In addition to these natural cycles, divinely ordained events were celebrated, based on the creation week – the sabbath and the seventh month – and the events of the deliverance from Egyptian bondage.

All these clearly foreshadowed the redemptive purpose of the Almighty. The seventh day of rest pointed forward to the Kingdom, when the redeemed enter the *"rest to the people of God"* (Heb. 4.9); and the Passover signified the freedom from bondage obtained by the offering of the Lamb of God. The Feast of Weeks looked forward to the firstfruits of Jew and Gentile believers; and the Feast of Tabernacles in the seventh month prefigured the rest and peace of the Kingdom when God's harvest will have been gathered in. Prior to this, on the first day of the seventh month had been the ritual of blowing of trumpets, symbolising the resurrection, followed by the Day of Atonement, which speaks of the final forgiveness of the redeemed.

All these regular celebrations were accompanied by various categories of animal offerings, as were an individual's need for atonement and forgiveness. These offerings, together with their generally accepted significance (see brackets in list below), pointed to the progressive stages of reconciliation to God, and are as follows:

- Sin offerings (forgiveness of sin nature)
- Trespass offerings (for specific sins)
- Burnt offerings (complete dedication to God)
- Peace offerings, or fellowship offerings (sharing future divine fellowship)

In keeping with this symbology, the first two were obligatory offerings – essential if the further stages of reconciliation were to be reached.

The future arrangements

These rituals and all these offerings – with presumably similar significances – will be reinstated in the future temple, albeit with some differences that we believe will reflect the altered situation applying in the millennium. As always, these are only personal and tentative suggestions.

Daily offerings

Under the Law of Moses two lambs had to be offered each day as a burnt offering, one in the morning and one in the evening (Num. 28.3-4). This offering was to be made irrespective of any additional offerings that may have been prescribed.

The meaning of this ordinance is clear – Israel was in continual need of forgiveness, and the daily sacrificial lamb pointed forward to the one who would ultimately achieve this. In the future a similar daily offering will be made, but only in the morning (Ezek. 46.13-15). Why will there be no evening sacrifice in the future?

There are three mentions of the evening sacrifice in the Old Testament, all of them associated with prayer and forgiveness: Elijah (1 Kgs 18.36); Ezra (Ezra 9.5); and David (Psa. 141.2). Thus that time of the day was possibly regarded as the "hour of prayer". This "hour of prayer" is stated in Acts 3.1 as being the ninth hour (3 pm in our reckoning of time), and Josephus says that this was the time that the evening sacrifice was offered (*Ant.* 14.4.3).

All the synoptic gospel records seem to stress the fact that the Lamb of God, of which these daily sacrifices were the type, died at this ninth hour

(Matt. 27.46,50, etc.), that is, at the very time that the evening sacrifice was being offered in the temple. Thus the evening sacrifice was especially associated with Christ's death. By the time of the millennium this will be a past event, and maybe this is the reason why this evening sacrifice will be omitted.

Sabbath offerings

Under the Law of Moses an additional morning and evening lamb was sacrificed on the sabbath (making two on each occasion; Num. 28.9). But in the future the sabbath offerings will be different. The evening sacrifice is again omitted, but for the morning offering Ezekiel mentions six lambs as burnt offerings and one ram as a peace offering (Ezek. 46.4). Again we ask the reason for the differences. As before, we can only make tentative suggestions.

The sabbath is a clear figure for the *"rest that remaineth"* (Heb. 4.9) and under the Mosaic system the doubling of the sacrificial lambs perhaps foretold that God's sacrificial lamb would result in the saving of two groups of people, Jews and Gentiles, who would enjoy that rest. (A similar doubling occurred in the Pentecost offering of the two barley loaves, which are generally reckoned to refer to God's harvest from both groups.)

A similar thought may explain the increased sabbath offerings in the millennium. As in the past there will be a daily requirement to highlight the need for atonement of the whole world – not now simply two groups, but a larger number of nations that will be turning to God and the things represented by the temple; indeed it will be a *"house of prayer for all nations"*. So could it be that the increased number of lambs reflects the greater number of nations in the millennium that will benefit from the atoning work of the Lamb of God?

The future inclusion of a peace offering on the sabbath may be understood in the light of its figurative significance. The distinguishing feature of a peace offering is that the offerer uses it to share a sacrificial meal – hence the concept of fellowship. In the millennium the long disrupted fellowship between God and man is being restored.

The new moons

Under the Law the start of every month had to be celebrated by the offering of two young bullocks, one ram, seven lambs as burnt offerings and one kid of the goats as a sin offering (Num. 28.11–15). In the future temple the new moon will be celebrated by a similar selection of animals, the main difference being that only one bullock will be offered, and no sin offering included (Ezek. 46.6).

Why only one bullock? A possible answer is that under the Law a bullock was sacrificed to represent one of two groups – either *"the priest that is anointed"* or the nation of Israel (Lev. 4.3,13). Thus on the Day of Atonement the high priest was represented by a bullock (Lev. 16.11). By the time of the millennium Christ will have already completed his sacrificial work, so only one of the two, Israel, will need to be represented, making one bullock appropriate.

No blowing of trumpets

One of the notable events in the Mosaic calendar was the blowing of trumpets on the first day of the seventh month (Lev. 23.24). This preceded the Day of Atonement on the tenth day and the Feast of Tabernacles from the fourteenth day onward. These clearly depict the sequence of events at the beginning of the millennium – resurrection (1 Thess. 4.16), forgiveness and then blessing. But by the time of the future temple, the first two of these stages will be in the past. So, there is no reference to the blowing of trumpets nor, as we note below, a Day of Atonement.

New Year's Day

The Law had no special offerings prescribed for the New Year, but in the future there will be a new ordinance. The first day of the year will be set aside as a special day of reconciliation, with its associated offerings: *"Thus saith the Lord GOD; In the first month, in the first day of the month, thou shalt take a young bullock without blemish, and cleanse the sanctuary: and the priest shall take of the blood of the sin offering, and put it upon the posts of the house, and upon the four corners of the settle of the altar, and upon the posts of the gate of the inner court"* (Ezek. 45.18–19).

This was to be repeated on the seventh day of the first month: *"for every one that erreth, and for him that is simple: so shall ye reconcile the house"* (v.20). The word translated "simple" has the underlying meaning of "to entice" or "deceive", in the sense that an erring one is deceived by sin – the NIV translating the verse as *"anyone who sins unintentionally or through ignorance"*.

One of the notable events in the Mosaic calendar was the Day of Atonement on the tenth day of the seventh month, when the sprinkled blood was taken into the most holy place for the forgiveness of the nation's sins. On that occasion the offerings were also one young bullock, together with other sacrifices. It is significant that in Ezekiel no mention is made of this Day of Atonement; indeed, there apparently will be no ark and mercy seat on which to sprinkle any blood. We therefore wonder if this future ceremony in the first week of a new year replaces the old ordinance on the tenth day of the seventh month. Maybe the Day of Atonement's earlier position, just a few days before the Feast of Tabernacles, would be inappropriate in the millennium. For by then the forgiveness symbolised by the Day of Atonement will have already been granted to the redeemed. But the mortal worshippers will still need to be reminded of the need for forgiveness, and the beginning of the year could be seen as appropriate for this, the offering of a single bullock representing the whole world.

Passover

The "restitution of all things" continues in the re-establishment of the Passover on the fourteenth day of the first month, and the following seven-day feast. But in the future there will be no roasted lamb to be eaten or a ritual of sprinkling its blood. This is understandable because the deliverance foretold by the exodus ritual will have been achieved. But, as before, unleavened bread is to be eaten for the seven days of the feast (Ezek. 45.21), maybe pointing to the personal discipline that will still be necessary in the worshippers.

Under the Law, on each of the seven days of this feast two bullocks, one ram, seven lambs and one goat were to be offered. This will vary in the future: the prince will offer one bullock – for himself; but for the people there will be seven bullocks offered each day (45.22–23), possibly indicating the greater number of nations in need of deliverance.

This ceremony again looks back to the redeeming work of Christ.

Feast of Firstfruits

Under the Law this commemorated the occasion when God spoke His law from heaven at Sinai (see also Acts 2.1–4), and involved the offering of two loaves. These typified the two groups of people, Jews and Gentiles, who would be the *"the firstfruits unto God and to the Lamb"* (Rev. 14.4). By the time of the millennium God's law will have *"gone forth from Zion"* and these two groups will already have been redeemed, so this may be the reason why Ezekiel does not include this feast.

Feast of Tabernacles

In the past, the fourteenth day of the seventh month was the commencement of a week of dwelling in booths: a symbol of the peace and rest of the Kingdom after the harvest had been gathered in. Alongside this, from the fifteenth day to the twenty-third day, was a series of offerings. The main feature of these was that each day the number of bullocks offered was reduced, leaving only one for the final day. If, as previously suggested, bullocks could represent a nation, this Mosaic provision foretold the gradual reduction in the number of individual nations as the Kingdom progressed.

In the future, when this time of peace will have actually come, this will be re-instituted, but again with some modifications. There is no reference to dwelling in booths, understandably, as the rest and peace they foretold will then be a reality (although there is a reference elsewhere to keeping the Feast of Tabernacles, Zech. 14.16). Nor will the decreasing number of bullocks be a feature, as only one group of nations needs to be represented. In fact the offerings for this week will be the same as for the Passover week: *"In the seventh month, in the fifteenth day of the month, shall he do the like in the feast of the seven days, according to the sin offering, according to the burnt offering, and according to the meat offering, and according to the oil"* (Ezek. 45.25).

Why these offerings?

There is no doubt that these offerings will take place in the future temple. Indeed, if they are considered to be inappropriate, then the whole point of having such a temple is negated. May we suggest three reasons that might make them pertinent to the future temple:

1. As mentioned before, they will remind the world of the sacrifice of Jesus, being a memorial of his great work of redemption.

2. In a previous chapter (see page 11) we suggested that the sacrificial offerings would be confined to the *"people of the land"*, primarily the restored nation of Israel (Ezek. 45.16,22; 46.3,9). We could not find any scriptural reference to the world at large engaging in such offerings – although its inhabitants clearly visit the temple and worship in it. If this is so, would Israel's particular obligation to offer sacrifices be a reminder to them of their specific guilt in crucifying their Messiah? They, of all the nations, needed forgiveness for what they did to Jesus. This special need for pardon may be suggested by the words of Zechariah. Israel will *"look upon me whom they have pierced"* (12.10) and *"in that day there shall be a fountain opened to the house of David and to the inhabitants of Jerusalem for sin and for uncleanness"* (13.1).

3. Just as in the past, the regular daily and weekly offerings pointed to the need for continual recognition of Israel's need for forgiveness and atonement; so in the future these offerings will extend that message to all the nations of the world. As suggested above, this may be the reason why the regular offerings are sometimes different from the previous system.

Other aspects of future worship

There are other references apart from those in Ezekiel which bear upon this study. Jeremiah speaks of *"them that shall bring the sacrifice of praise into the house of the LORD"* (33.11). No doubt this temple will be the focus of worldwide honour and praise to the Almighty. But Malachi speaks of a worship that will not be confined to the temple: *"For from the rising of the sun even unto the going down of the same my name shall be great among the Gentiles; and in every place incense shall be offered unto my name, and a pure offering: for my name shall be great among the heathen, saith the LORD of hosts"* (1.11).

Another notable feature of past and future temple worship is the activities of singers. These were a dominant aspect of the worship instituted under divine control by Samuel (1 Chron. 9.33), David and Solomon, and it is certain that singers will have an important place in future temple services (Ezek. 40.44), although we are not told any details. Another aspect for future worship is that, as in the past (1 Kgs 8.41–43), all nations will be invited to pray to the God who will dwell in this glorious *"house of prayer"* (Isa. 56.7)

The suggestions in this chapter are only tentative, and highlight our own lack of understanding of these future arrangements. As with so many prophecies, the main outline is clear but the details are uncertain. The foregoing is submitted with this proviso, and in the hope of soon experiencing the realities of this future time.

Chapter 12 The living waters: geographical changes

The perennial stream issuing from the temple has already been mentioned (Chapter 7), but it is such an important feature of the new sanctuary that it deserves a closer look. In this chapter we will consider the provision of literal water, but throughout we should keep in mind that all this has symbolic applications. The book of Revelation raises the literal waters of Ezekiel to a spiritual dimension: *"And he shewed me a pure river of water of life, clear as crystal, proceeding out of the throne of God and of the Lamb … and on either side of the river, was there the tree of life, which bare twelve manner of fruits, and yielded her fruit every month: and the leaves of the tree were for the healing of the nations"* (22.1-2).

Here is the promise of eternal life, as Jesus had foretold: *"Let him that is athirst come. And whosoever will, let him take the water of life freely"* (Rev. 22.17); *"The water that I shall give him shall be in him a well of water springing up into everlasting life"* (John 4.14). But, possibly to re-enforce this message, literal healing waters will in the future also flow out from the divine presence.

The source and direction of the water

Having completed his measurements and descriptions of the entire range of buildings, Ezekiel's guide brought the prophet back into the inner court, on the west side of which was the façade of the temple building. Here he saw a cascade of water issuing from under its foundations: *"Afterward he brought me back to the door of the temple; and behold, water was issuing from below the threshold of the temple toward the east (for the temple faced east); and the water was flowing down from below the south end of the threshold of the temple, south of the altar"* (Ezek. 47.1, RSV).

The source of this living water is important (see Figure 15). As in Revelation, symbology, so in the future, reality. The water will come directly from the temple, the building from which Ezekiel had heard the awesome words: *"Son of man, the place of my throne, and the place of the soles of my feet, where I will dwell in the midst of the children of Israel for ever"* (43.7). So here is water emanating from the very presence of the Almighty. Then will the Psalmist's words have their complete fulfilment: *"There is a river, the streams whereof shall make glad the city of God, the holy place of the tabernacles of the most High. God is in the midst of her; she shall not be moved"* (Psa. 46.4–5).

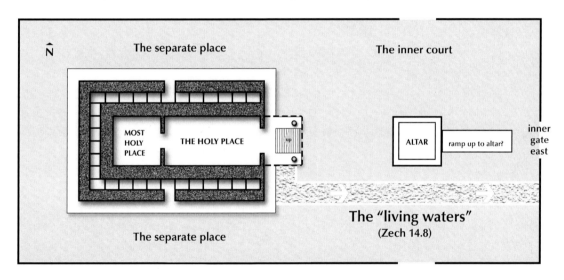

Figure 15 The source of the "living waters".

It seems that Ezekiel saw this water flowing across the inner court on the south side of the centrally placed altar of burnt offering. We suggested earlier that this living, or running, water will take the place of the Mosaic laver, and will be where the priests wash before carrying out their duties.

Although it is not specifically mentioned, on its outward path the water probably flowed out across the outer courtyard as well, in the vicinity of the outer east gate. We have already noted (chapter 10) that this gate was permanently shut (44.1), so this is why Ezekiel's guide had to lead him out through the north gate in order to follow the course of the waters as they left the sanctuary: *"Then he brought me out by way of the north gate, and led me round on the outside to the outer gate, that faces toward the east; and the water was coming out on the south side"* (47.2, RSV). As the next verse indicates, the water then proceeded in an easterly direction.

A deepening river

Ezekiel's guide then made a series of measurements along the eastward course of what had now become a river: *"And when the man that had the line in his hand went forth eastward, he measured a thousand cubits, and he brought me through the waters; the waters were to the ankles. Again he measured a thousand, and brought me through the waters; the waters were to the knees. Again he measured a thousand, and brought me through; the waters were to the loins. Afterward he measured a thousand; and it was a river that I could not pass over: for the waters were risen, waters to swim in, a river that could not be passed over"* (47.3–5).

What will cause this flow of water – originally a comparatively small stream – to become *"a river that could not be passed over"*? How will Jerusalem, *"the city of our solemnities"*, become *"a place of broad rivers and streams"* (Isa. 33.20–21)? This is possibly answered by other prophecies relating to these times, and we will make a somewhat extensive digression to consider their impact on the future scene. We stress that the following are only suggestions that *may* be a way in which some of the admittedly obscure prophecies could be fulfilled.

84

Future earthquakes

A consistent theme of the end-time prophecies is that the land of Israel will experience huge earthquakes. Isaiah speaks of: *"the glory of his majesty, when he ariseth to shake terribly the earth"* (2.19); Ezekiel predicts that: *"in that day there shall be a great shaking in the land of Israel … and all the men that are upon the face of the earth, shall shake at my presence, and the mountains shall be thrown down, and the steep places shall fall, and every wall shall fall to the ground"* (38.19-20); and Joel foresaw that: *"The LORD also shall roar out of Zion, and utter his voice from Jerusalem; and the heavens and the earth shall shake"* (3.16).

Geologists confirm that the whole area of the Middle East is unstable and very prone to earthquakes, especially in the Jordan valley. One writer, under the heading "A Disaster Foretold" says: "Today, next week or in fifty years, a massive earthquake will devastate Israel. And Israel, say the experts, is no better prepared than New Orleans was for a catastrophe sure to come. From Jerusalem, the Hashemite Kingdom of Jordan doesn't appear to be going anywhere. It sits where it has for as long as anyone can remember, across the rumpled wastelands of the Jordan Valley to the east, its slopes rising to a desert plateau. But every year Jordan moves, on average, four-fifths of an inch to the north, slipping along the fault line that runs through the valley, which is part of the larger cleft in the earth's surface known as the Syrian-African Rift" (*Jerusalem Report*, 17 Oct. 2005). When the tension built up by this slippage is released a devastating earthquake will result.

The Mount of Olives split

One such earthquake that relates specifically to Jerusalem is prophesied by Zechariah. After describing the final battle at Jerusalem, when God *"shall go forth, and fight against those nations, as when he fought in the day of battle"*, he predicts: *"And his feet shall stand in that day upon the mount of Olives, which is before Jerusalem on the east, and the mount of Olives shall cleave in the midst thereof toward the east and toward the west, and there shall be a very great valley; and half of the mountain shall remove toward the north, and half of it toward the south. And ye shall flee to [by, NIV] the valley of the mountains; for the valley of the mountains shall reach unto Azal: yea, ye shall flee, like as ye fled from before the earthquake in the days of Uzziah king of Judah"* (14.3–5).

So here is a clear prophecy that the Mount of Olives will experience an east/west split to form a large valley. Such a phenomenon is not unknown in geological history. The following is a comment on a similar event elsewhere about a hundred years ago: "The cleaving in two of the Mount of Olives in Zechariah 14.4 is regarded by most commentators as being quite beyond a literal interpretation: and yet, a few years ago *The Illustrated London News* gave some interesting drawings of the scene of the great volcanic eruption in the North Island, New Zealand. It will be remembered that the outburst of volcanic energy began by the explosion of Mount Tarawera, a mountain which had no crater upon it, and showed no signs of recent activity. Tarawera *was split in two* by the sudden opening of a great chasm or line of craters four miles long, about 500 feet wide, and, in many places, 400 feet deep" (E.W. Bullinger, *The Apocalypse*, 1909).

Initially an escape route

In Zechariah the Hebrew word for "valley" is the one used to describe a "steep valley, narrow gorge" (*Strong's*), as distinct from another word that describes a broader valley. Along this new narrow valley some refugees from Jerusalem will escape the terrors in the city resulting from the northern invasion.

The comparison with a previous earthquake in Uzziah's day is interesting, for that was such a notable event that it stood out as a landmark in

Jerusalem's history. Amos dates his prophecy by it (1.1) and it was still remembered hundreds of years later in the days of Zechariah. Josephus describes how "a great earthquake shook the ground ... and before the city, at a place called Eroge half the mountain broke off from the rest, and rolled itself four furlongs, till the roads, as well as the king's gardens, were spoiled by the obstruction" (*History of the Jews*, 9.10.4). Archaeological evidence for this earthquake in Amos's day has been uncovered, the damage suggesting a huge convulsion indeed – estimated at about 8 on the Richter scale.

The future quake will be even more devastating, resulting (among other changes to be considered later) in a valley that will reach right up to the eastern side of Jerusalem. This is suggested by the statement that this new valley will *"reach unto Azal"*. Concerning this Azal, *Speaker's Commentary* says that it is "the name probably of some suburb of Jerusalem on the eastern side, and at the western entrance of the valley of escape. It may be identical with the Beth-ezel of Micah 1.11, which seems from verse 12 to have been near one of the gates of Jerusalem. The derivation of the word from *atzel,* 'to lean upon', 'to incline to', may suggest a slope from the city gate by which the fugitives were to escape into the valley, and then Beth-ezel would be the buildings on that slope."

But by the time the temple is in operation the trauma of the future Gogian attack of Ezekiel 38–39 will be over, and, instead of being an escape route for Jerusalem's inhabitants, the valley will probably form the course of the living waters issuing from the temple.

Water of increasing depth

If this new valley, extending right up to the eastern boundary of Jerusalem, were to have a slightly upward sloping floor as it went away from the city, the very situation described in Ezekiel would be met. The waters would get progressively deeper until the highest point of the valley floor was reached (which would possibly be beyond the deepest point described by Ezekiel), after which they would cascade away down to the Jordan valley. The river would also get progressively wider to cover the width of the new valley, producing a lake at least 3000 cubits (one mile or 1.6 km) long, but probably longer – *"broad rivers and streams"* indeed, but because of its elevated position, impossible for a *"galley with oars"* or *"gallant ship"* to navigate (Isa. 33.21).

Is it possible that this stretch of water will be used to baptise the newly-converted people who come to worship the Almighty in the temple? Archaeologists excavating the temple of Christ's day found at the eastern entrance large baths for the purification of the incoming worshippers, and this waterway, also to the east of the new temple, could have a similar purpose in the future.

The continuing course of the river

The subsequent course of this new river is more precisely mentioned by the prophets: *"These waters issue out toward the east country, and go down into the desert, and go into the sea"* (Ezek. 47.8). *"A fountain shall come forth of the house of the LORD, and shall water the valley of Shittim"* (Joel 3.18). The valley of Shittim is the Jordan valley in the region of Jericho (Num. 25.1; Josh. 3.1; Mic. 6.5), and *"the sea"* of Ezekiel is clearly the Dead Sea. So this is apparently straightforward: the river goes down directly to the Jordan valley, having the effects that we will consider later.

A divided waterway

But a reference in Zechariah adds another dimension: *"On that day living water will flow out from Jerusalem, **half** to the eastern sea and **half** to the western sea, in summer and in winter"* (14.8, NIV). The *"eastern sea"* is clearly the Dead Sea, into which the water can obviously flow directly; but the *"western sea"* is the Mediterranean. So in some way the water that flows from the temple eastwards through the new valley will end up in the Mediterranean Sea as well as in the Dead Sea. This presents a geographical problem, for the two seas are separated by an extensive range of 900 metre (3000 feet) high hills running north to south, with no valley crossing them in the vicinity of Jerusalem that the new river could use. We suggest two possible answers to this dilemma.

A major topographical change

First, geological changes are predicted for this area, which could open up a new access to the Mediterranean for part of this new river. For as well as the splitting of the mount of Olives, other huge changes will take place: *"The whole land, from Geba to Rimmon, south of Jerusalem, will become like the Arabah. But Jerusalem will be raised up and remain in its place, from the Benjamin Gate to the site of the First Gate, to the Corner Gate, and from the Tower of Hananel to the royal winepresses"* (Zech. 14. 10, NIV). After locating Geba and Rimmon the size of this lowered area becomes apparent.

Geba was a town about four miles north of Jerusalem, and under the kings was the most northern town of the territory of the kingdom of Judah. The whole of Judah's territory was in fact described as *"from Geba to Beersheba"* (2 Kgs 23.8).

There is more than one Rimmon mentioned in Scripture, but only one was sited "south of Jerusalem". It is listed in Joshua 15 as being one of *"the southernmost towns of the tribe of Judah in the Negev towards the boundary of Edom"* (vv.21,32, NIV). It was in the hill country of Judah, about ten miles north of Beersheba.

If the identification of these places is correct, Zechariah describes an immense geological change that will take place in Israel. The *"whole land"*, from 4 miles north of Jerusalem to about 36 miles south of the city, will be altered. At present this area contains hills much higher than Jerusalem – to the north near Geba they rise to about 850 metres (2800 feet) compared with Jerusalem's 760 metres (2500 feet), and to the south near Hebron they rise to well over 900 metres (3000 feet). But this whole area, with the exception of Jerusalem, is to *"become like the Arabah"*.

The "Arabah" is the term consistently used in Scripture to delineate the deep rift valley of the Jordan, but in what sense the newly affected area will come to resemble it is not clear. It may be a reference (confirmed by the KJV translation of *arabah* as "plain") to the flatness of that valley's bottom, suggesting that all the hills to the north and south of Jerusalem will be levelled out and reduced in height. Thus Jerusalem will become the prominent feature of the area. This is in line with Micah's prediction: *"It shall come to pass in the latter days that the mountain of the house of the LORD shall be established as **the highest of the mountains, and shall be raised up above the hills**"* (4.1, RSV). Presumably this will also lower the height of the Mount of Olives, but this should not affect the suggestions made earlier.

Reverting to the question of how one arm of the divided living waters reaches the Mediterranean, a colleague who is familiar with the area points out that the valley of Rephaim, west of Jerusalem, leading down to the valley of Sorek (currently the route of the railway line from the coast up to the city) could be a possible route for this arm of the new river. He points out that this was the area of David's conquest of the idolatrous Philistines and of Samson's exploits. A cleansing watercourse in this area, draining out into the Mediterranean, would in symbol purge away those emblems of sin and uncleanness.

Or it could be that the great topographical changes will open up a new route for the western flowing arm of the river. What at present seems impractical could then be easily achieved once these topographical changes have occurred.

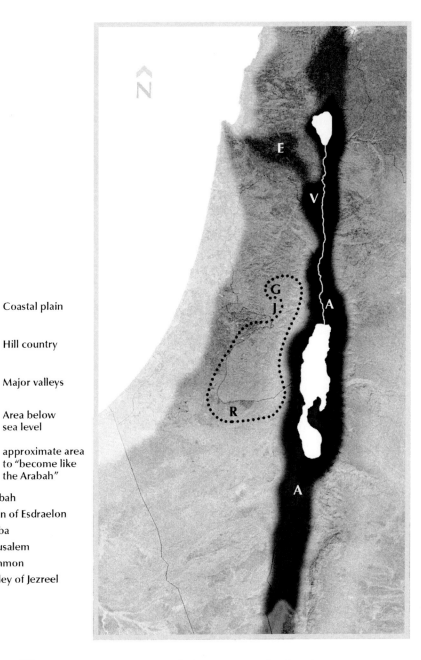

KEY

Coastal plain

Hill country

Major valleys

Area below
sea level

••••• approximate area
to "become like
the Arabah"

A = Arabah
E = Plain of Esdraelon
G = Geba
J = Jerusalem
R = Rimmon
V = Valley of Jezreel

Figure 16 Future topographical changes to the land.

Another route to the Mediterranean

But there is another possible way in which Zechariah's prediction of a waterway extending to the Great Sea will come to pass. The Dead Sea, as is well known, is situated in the Great Rift Valley that runs down to the Gulf of Aqaba. The sea's surface is over 400 metres (1300 feet) below the level of the Mediterranean and in its stifling heat the water from the Jordan evaporates as fast as it flows in. The consequent salt build-up makes the water virtually lifeless.

But all this is to change when the healing waters from the temple reach this area: *"And he said to me, This water flows toward the eastern region and goes down into the Arabah ... and will become fresh. And wherever the river goes every living creature which swarms will live, and there will be very many fish; for this water goes there, that the waters of the sea may become fresh; so everything will live where the river goes"* (47.8-9, RSV).

At present the whole of the Jordan valley, including the Sea of Galilee and the Dead Sea, is below normal sea level (see Figure 16). A new and copious supply of water would flood the whole area to form a long narrow lake stretching from just north of the Sea of Galilee to well beyond the southern tip of the Dead Sea (incidentally, sending Capurnaum "down to hades", Matt. 11.23). Where would the water then go? For the whole area is almost completely surrounded by hills, and the southern part of the Arabah rises to nearly 300 metres (1000 feet) before dropping away again to the Gulf of Aqaba.

There is just one possible escape route – the point where the valley of Jezreel feeds into the Jordan valley. Most of the valley of Jezreel is below sea level (see Figure 16), and its western end is only a short distance from the source of the river Kishon that now flows down across the Plain of Esdraelon and out to the Mediterranean. Thus this valley, when flooded along with the rest of the Jordan valley, could be the natural outlet for the waters descending from Jerusalem. This would be in keeping with what Zechariah says: that half of the waters will go to heal the Dead Sea, and the rest proceed out to the Mediterranean; and this could be by way of the valley of Jezreel and the Plain of Esdraelon.

Fishermen at En-gedi

But this suggestion does not immediately fit another reference in Ezekiel 47. Referring to the Dead Sea we read: *"Fishermen will stand beside the sea; from En-gedi to En-eglaim it will be a place for the spreading of nets; its fish will be of very many kinds, like the fish of the Great Sea. But its swamps and marshes will not become fresh; they are to be left for salt"* (vv.10–11, RSV).

If the present Jordan valley were to be filled up to about the level of the Mediterranean, as envisaged above, then the current site of En-gedi would be buried under the water, and there would not be adjacent marshy areas to be used as a salt supply. But it has been suggested that the huge subsidence causing the reduction in the height of the Judean hills will possibly be accompanied by a compensating rise in the Dead Sea area. This could raise this region sufficiently to preserve the places and features mentioned by Ezekiel.

Trees for food and health

Whatever the physical details, we must never overlook the immense benefits that will accrue from this "living water" supplied by a beneficent Creator to His people. The new stream will transform the whole area, bringing life to a previously barren landscape. Ezekiel specifically mentions the life-giving trees that will line the course of this new waterway – trees that will have unique qualities because they will be irrigated by water from such a holy source: *"And by the river upon the bank thereof, on this side and on that side, shall grow all trees for meat, whose leaf shall not fade, neither shall the fruit thereof be consumed: it shall bring forth new fruit according to his months, because their waters they issued out of the sanctuary: and the fruit thereof shall be for meat, and the leaf thereof for medicine"* (47.12). One can imagine the delight, anticipation and thankfulness with which the visitors to the temple will eat this constant supply of food and healing medicine.

Only suggestions

As with so many as yet unfulfilled prophecies, we can only make suggestions as to how they might come to pass. The reality will probably be vastly different from anything that we can envisage. But the prophecies are all part of the inspired Word given for our instruction, and such details as we have examined would presumably not have been given if its readers were not intended to study and think about them. May such considerations strengthen our faith in God's holy Word and increase our longing to share in these delightful times.

Chapter 13 **The division of the land**

After showing Ezekiel the "living waters" that proceeded from the temple, his guide went on to delineate how the land of Israel was to be apportioned in the future. Unlike when Israel first settled in the land and had irregular tribal boundaries, the tribes will be regularly spaced out in equal allocations (Ezek. 47.14). But, as we will see, the overall area that Israel will possess is very similar, if not identical, to that occupied in the past. As in all this study there are aspects that cannot be decided with any certainty, and the following is offered with this proviso.

The northern boundary

First, the extent of the land is outlined, starting with the north border: *"This shall be the boundary of the land: On the north side, from the Great Sea by way of Hethlon to Lebo-hamath, and on to Zedad, Berothah, Sibraim (which lies between the border of Damascus and the border of Hamath), as far as Hazer-hatticon, which is on the border of Hauran. So the boundary shall run from the sea to Hazar-enon, which is north of the border of Damascus, with the border of Hamath to the north. This shall be the north side"* (Ezek. 47.15–17, NIV).

Comparing these boundaries with those given by Moses, and allocated by Joshua on Israel's first entry into the land, we find several place names are common to both descriptions: *"And this shall be your north border: from the great sea ye shall point out for you mount Hor: from mount Hor ye shall point out your border unto the entrance of Hamath; and the goings forth of the border shall be to Zedad: and the border shall go on to Ziphron, and the goings out of it shall be at Hazar-enan: this shall be your north border"* (Num. 34.7–9). From the inclusion of the *"border* ["lebo" or

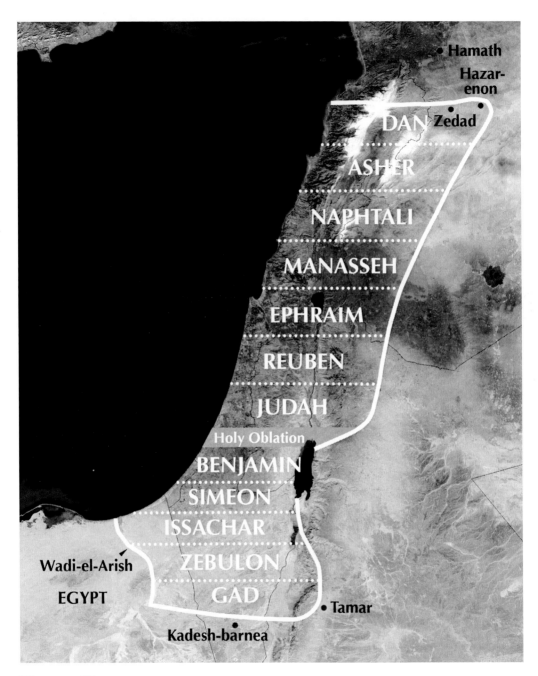

Figure 17 The division of the land

96

"entrance"] *of Hamath"*, *"Zedad"* and *"Hazar-enan"*, it is clear that a similar boundary is being described in both records.

Whilst not all the places are identifiable today, some can be located with a degree of certainty (see Figure 17). Hamath was the capital city of a nation of that same name; the *"entering in of Hamath"* refers to the start of the valley leading up to that city, and is often used to describe the northern-most boundary of Israel (Num. 13.21; 1 Kings 8.65; 2 Kings 14.25). Thus in old times the northern boundary went eastward from the Great Sea, across the valley leading to Hamath. It continued to Zedad – "clearly identical with Sadad, a village on the road between Ribleh and Qaryetain" (*International Standard Bible Encyclopedia*, ISBE), near to the northern boundary of the territory of Damascus. Ezekiel clearly depicts a similar route for the future northern boundary.

The eastern boundary

Having located the northern border, Ezekiel was given a line southward from its eastern corner down to a place called "Tamar": *"On the east side the boundary shall run from Hazar-enon, between Hauran and Damascus; along the Jordan between Gilead and the land of Israel; to the eastern sea and as far as Tamar. This shall be the east side"* (Ezek. 47.18, RSV). Hauran is the area: "from Dan in the North to Gilead in the South, including all that lay between the Jordan and the desert" (ISBE). It is still known by this name, and by the Greeks and Romans as "Auranitis".

So the boundary proceeds south by way of *"Gilead"*, the *"land of Israel"*, down to the *"eastern sea"* (Dead Sea). These first two places are presumably mentioned so as to include the trans-Jordan area occupied by the two and a half tribes, but which were not delineated by Moses in Numbers 34 because the circumstances surrounding their allocation had not yet arrived. The reference to the boundary going *"along the Jordan"* might seem to exclude these two areas, but why are they mentioned at all if the border simply follows the course of the Jordan? In fact the word for "along" is not in the original text, making the meaning rather unclear.

The eastern boundary ends at Tamar, south of the Dead Sea. According to Eusebius, Tamar was a village with a Roman garrison on the way from Hebron to Elath, which is at the southern end of the "Arabah". Ptolemy also mentions Tamar under the name Thamaro, on the road from Hebron to Petra, but its precise location is unknown.

The southern boundary

This runs westward from Tamar to the Great Sea along the river valley termed in the KJV *"the river of Egypt"*: *"On the south side, it shall run from Tamar as far as the waters of Meribah kadesh, from there along the Wadi* [river, KJV] *of Egypt to the Great Sea. This shall be the south side"* (v. 19, NIV). The waters of Meribah locate the site of Israel's failure in the wilderness (Exod. 17.1–7), usually associated with Kadesh-Barnea, whose traditional location is to the extreme south of the territory of Israel (Josh. 15.23, RSV).

The "river of Egypt"

Scholars have been divided over the identification of this scriptural term. The KJV's *"river of Egypt"*, has been taken to describe either the River Nile or a smaller seasonal stream that flows into the Mediterranean about fifty miles south of Gaza. Examination of the original terms for "river" probably suggests what sort of watercourse is intended. The Hebrew word *nahar* describes a river in our accepted sense – a flowing stream of moving water. Rivers such as the Euphrates and the Nile are described by this term. But the *"river of Egypt"* uses a different word, *nachal*, which conveys the idea of a "torrent", and is used to describe the usually dry valleys through which water cascades in times of flood. Its modern equivalent is the Arabic wadi, which refers not only to the seasonal stream but also to the valley bed itself. There is such a watercourse to the south of Israel, the Wadi-el-Arish, that runs from what is called the Sinai Peninsula to the Mediterranean Sea, and it is this wadi that formed the southern boundary of Israel (Num. 34.5; Josh. 15.47; 1 Kings 8.65, etc.). In these frequent references to *"the river of Egypt"* it is not *the* river of Egypt, the Nile, that is being described, but most likely this Wadi-el-Arish, which formed the natural political boundary between Israel and Egypt. Indeed, the terms *"river of Egypt"* and *"border of Egypt"* are used interchangeably in the parallel records of 1 Kings 4.21 and 2 Chronicles 9.26. That the southern boundary of Israel was indeed along the Wadi-el-Arish is also often referred to in external writings relating to this time.

The old boundaries restored

The future western boundary of the land will be the same as that originally mentioned by Moses: the Mediterranean Sea (Num. 34.6; Ezek. 47.20).

It is therefore evident that in the future the boundaries of the restored nation of Israel will be very similar to those that Israel actually possessed after the Exodus (although then the area was less than God originally intended; it could have extended to the Euphrates (Gen. 15.18; Deut. 1.7; Josh. 1.3–4).

The tribal allocations

Ezekiel 48 describes the arrangement of the twelve tribes within the boundaries just outlined; but the apparently straightforward disposition of the territory is not without its problems. Each is to have a strip of land *"extending from the east side to the west"* (v.1, RSV), starting with the tribe of Dan next to the northern boundary. South of Dan will be the portion for Asher, followed by those of Naphtali, Manasseh, Ephraim, Reuben and Judah.

South of the portion for Judah is a strip of land in which is the "holy oblation", containing the temple and the possession of its ministers, with the prince's portion on either side – a feature that warrants a separate chapter. South of the holy oblation the remaining five tribes have their portions: Benjamin, Simeon, Issachar, Zebulun and Gad.

We have tried without success to uncover a reason for this particular sequence in Ezekiel. Indeed, looking at all the occasions when the twelve tribes are mentioned in Scripture (and there are about 24 such lists, all giving the tribes in a different order) it is difficult to establish a reason for the variations.

The overall north/south length of the area delineated is about 260 miles (420 km), and subtracting the given dimensions of the holy oblation, and assuming that the strips are equal, the width of each strip north of the holy oblation would be about 30 miles from north to south. South of that area, five tribes are fitted into the remaining 60 or so miles between the holy oblation and the Wadi-el-Arish, and would therefore have smaller dimensions from north to south.

God's promise to Abraham

It will be convenient now to return to *"the river of Egypt"* and note the single occasion where it could be taken as referring to the River Nile. When making His promise to Abraham God said: *"In the same day the LORD made a covenant with Abram, saying, Unto thy seed have I given this land, from the river of Egypt unto the great river, the river Euphrates: the Kenites, and the Kenizzites, and the Kadmonites, and the Hittites, and the Perizzites, and the Rephaims, and the Amorites, and the Canaanites, and the Girgashites, and the Jebusites"* (Gen. 15.18–21). Here the word in *"river of Egypt"* is *nahar*, the true river, rather than *nachal*, the wadi with its seasonal streams. Because of this it is thought by many, quite understandably, that when the promise is finally fulfilled Abraham's seed will inherit Egypt in the south and all the territory up to the Euphrates in the north. But, as we have seen, Ezekiel's northern boundary does not extend up to the Euphrates, so do we also need to have a different understanding of its extending into Egypt in the future?

The following points have been advanced in favour of the understanding that the *"river of Egypt"* is the Wadi-el-Arish and that this will therefore be the future southern boundary:

1. In most of later allusions to the fulfilment of the promise to Abraham, only the land of Canaan is being referred to (Gen. 12.5–7; 13.12–17; Exod. 6.4–8; Deut 34.1–4; Neh. 9.8). This is in line with God's elaboration of the promise in Genesis 15, listing the Canaanite tribes that were to be displaced. Why mention only those if a much wider area was intended?

2. The River Nile was a greater river than the Euphrates. Why, then, did God only describe the latter as being "great"? Was it to make a contrast with the small wadi?

3. Israel clearly departed from Egypt under Moses, and there is no scriptural or historical evidence that they later inherited any part of the country they had left behind.

But others suggest that rather than indicating the main river, the Nile, the eastern branch of its delta was meant by the term *"river of Egypt"*. They point out that whilst mentioning the Euphrates by name, God, by contrast, did not use the well-known specific word for the River Nile, *Ye'or*, but *nahar*, the general term for a river. The suggestion is that the Pelucian arm of the Nile, the most easterly channel in the delta, is the *"river of Egypt"*; and this enters the Mediterranean further south than the Wadi-el-Arish.

If this slightly southerly location of the *"river of Egypt"* is accepted, then it means that Israel in the future will have a small foothold on Egyptian territory. This would then mean that the future boundary of the twelve tribes would be extended considerably westwards, thus fulfilling part of the terms of God's promise in Genesis 15. If this were so, it would mean that the five tribes south of the temple could have approximately the same areas as those to the north. But even then the other detail of the promise, concerning a possession up to the Euphrates, would still not be met.

The future Solomon

The answer may lie in the situation in the days of David and Solomon, a recognised type of Christ's future Kingdom. In those days Israel's empire extended beyond the boundaries allocated by Moses and settled under Joshua. Of Solomon we read: *"And Solomon reigned over all kingdoms from the river* [i.e. Euphrates] *unto the land of the Philistines, and unto the border* [nachal] *of Egypt: they brought presents, and served Solomon all the days of his life"* (1 Kgs 4.21). But, although ruled by Solomon, not all of this large area was populated by the twelve tribes. They had inherited just the central section of this territory, as the passage continues: *"And Judah and Israel dwelt safely, every man under his vine and under his fig tree, from Dan even to Beer-sheba, all the days of Solomon"* (v.25).

So Solomon's dominion extended from Egypt to the Euphrates, and within that, from Dan to Beer-sheba, was the smaller portion for the twelve tribes. Was this a foretaste of the future, when Israel will be the central component of a larger group of nations?

This could be so. In fact the two extremities of the future domain, Egypt and Assyria, are the subject of a most enlightening prophecy that may have a bearing on the future situation: *"And the LORD shall be known to*

Egypt, and the Egyptians shall know the LORD in that day, and shall do sacrifice and oblation; yea, they shall vow a vow unto the LORD, and perform it. And the LORD shall smite Egypt: he shall smite and heal it: and they shall return even to the LORD, and he shall be intreated of them, and shall heal them. In that day shall there be a highway out of Egypt to Assyria, and the Assyrian shall come into Egypt, and the Egyptian into Assyria, and the Egyptians shall serve with the Assyrians. In that day shall Israel be the third with Egypt and with Assyria, even a blessing in the midst of the land: whom the LORD of hosts shall bless, saying, Blessed be Egypt my people, and Assyria the work of my hands, and Israel mine inheritance" (Isa. 19.21–25).

So in the Kingdom, when the promise to Abraham will be finally fulfilled, there will be three equal partners: Assyria (represented by the Euphrates in God's promise of Gen. 15.18), Egypt (represented by the river of Egypt) and Israel – all of them then regarded as God's people and His inheritance.

This chapter has gone well beyond the initial discussion of the tribal inheritance detailed by Ezekiel, but so often the study of the Word leads us into unexpected places. We have the picture of three nations in harmony and peace in the future: Assyria in the north, Israel in the centre – now settled in their tribal areas within the limits specified by Ezekiel as a *"blessing in the midst of the land"* – and Egypt in the south. The prospect of nations now so mutually antagonistic being united in obedience and service to God is one that provokes earnest anticipation by the watchers in Zion.

Chapter 14 **The holy oblation**

In the future division of the land, interspersed between the tribal allocations of Judah and Benjamin, will be an area termed in the KJV the "holy oblation", in which the sanctuary will be situated (Ezek. 45.1-6; 48.8-20). This holy portion of the land will be donated by all the tribes, Ezekiel's guide describing it as: *"The oblation that ye shall offer unto the LORD"* (48.9). The Hebrew word for "oblation" is the one usually applied to the offerings under the Law of Moses, particularly the heave offerings, in which a portion of the animal was ceremonially lifted up heavenwards. The same word is used in chapter 45.13 to describe the future produce offerings that Israel will make. So this area will be Israel's gift to God, holy and dedicated to His service.

Figure 18 The holy oblation.

The area thus offered to God will have precise dimensions: *"All the oblation shall be five and twenty thousand by five and twenty thousand: ye shall offer the holy oblation foursquare"* (48.20). As in some other cases, the unit of measurement is not specified in this passage, although in chapter 45.2-3, which also describes the holy oblation, the only units mentioned in the same context are cubits. This question of size was fully discussed in Chapter 3 and we believe that the dimensions of the holy oblation are measured in cubits. In modern measurements the length of each side of this holy square will be about 13.25 km (8.3 miles), giving a total area of 175 km² (69 square miles).

Figure 19 shows this square tract of land divided into three distinct areas: portions for **(a)** the priests, **(b)** the Levites, and **(c)** "the city" (45.5–6). These are described respectively as the *"most holy"*, the *"holy"* and the *"profane"* (Heb. *chol*, "common"), a clear analogy with the divisions of the tabernacle and temple and their related teaching, as we will consider later.

The "most holy" priests' portion

This is mentioned first, adjoining the territory of Judah to the north, and will be a 10,000 cubit strip extending across the 25,000 cubit northern boundary of the oblation (48.10). This area alone is described as an offering *"unto the LORD"* (45.1; 48.9), presumably because the sanctuary at Jerusalem will be within it. Emphasis is placed on the sanctity of this area; all the oblation will be holy, but this part especially so: *"And it shall belong to them as a special portion from the holy portion of the land, a most holy place, adjoining the territory of the Levites"* (48.12, RSV). Thus this tract of land will become the most holy spot on earth, described by the Almighty as: *"the place of my throne, and the place of the soles of my feet, where I will dwell in the midst of the children of Israel for ever"* (43.7).

Appropriately, this portion will be: *"for the priests that are sanctified of the sons of Zadok; which have kept my charge, which went not astray when the children of Israel went astray, as the Levites went astray"* (48.11). These are the mortal priests that will be allowed into the inner parts of the sanctuary; in contrast to the Levites, who will only minister in the outer court. In previous times, unlike the rest of the tribes, the Levitical priests did not have their own tracts of land but were given cities among the territories of the other tribes (Deut. 18.1–2). In the future they will have this piece of land for their exclusive use for houses and fields (Ezek. 45.4).

The "holy" Levites' portion

Next to the "most holy" portion, and of equal size, will be the territory of the Levites: *"And over against the border of the priests the Levites shall have five and twenty thousand in length, and ten thousand in breadth: all the length shall be five and twenty thousand, and the breadth ten thousand"* (48.13). This is referred to in chapter 45.6 as the "holy portion". Here the Levites will have their houses and fields, but because this is a holy portion it will not be permissible for them to sell the land or its

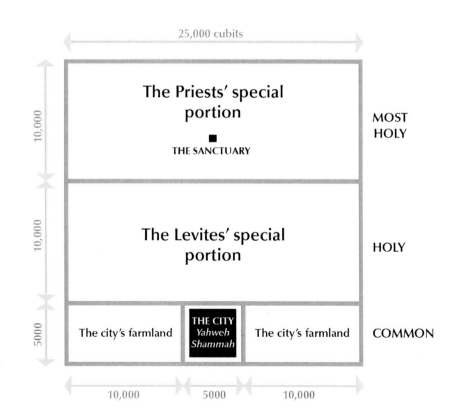

Figure 19

Details of the holy oblation.

produce: *"And they shall not sell of it, neither exchange, nor alienate* [Heb. to "pass over", i.e. to pass on to another] *the firstfruits of the land: for it is holy unto the LORD"* (48.14).

There is an interesting reference in chapter 45.5 regarding this portion: *"The Levites, the ministers of the house, have for themselves, for a possession for twenty chambers"*. Some other versions, based upon the Septuagint manuscripts, translate the last phrase as *"their possession for cities to live in"* (e.g. RSV). We thought that maybe the Dead Sea Scrolls might give a pointer to the correct rendering, but Professor Emanuel Tov, editor-in-chief of the scrolls at the Hebrew University, Jerusalem, has said that Ezekiel chapter 45 is not included in the fragments so far discovered.

It is accepted by many scholars that the KJV is correct. The Hebrew manuscripts use the word that is correctly translated as "chambers" elsewhere in Ezekiel, being used repeatedly for the rooms in the sanctuary. It would seem, therefore, that here there is an allusion to the allocation to the Levites of some of the outer court chambers that Ezekiel saw on his tour of the temple: *"Then brought he me into the outward court, and, lo, there were chambers, and a pavement made for the court round about: thirty chambers were upon the pavement"* (40.17). In the earlier temples there were chambers of the Levites designed to receive the tithes offered by the nation (Num. 18.21; 1 Chron. 9.26; Neh. 10.37), and it seems that of the thirty chambers in the outer court of the future temple, twenty will be used by the Levites for this purpose, to store the *"firstfruits of the land"* (48.14).

A greater inheritance

It might be felt that this future allocation for the priests and Levites is small in comparison with that of the rest of the tribes. But in fact it will be considerably greater than their possessions under the Law of Moses. Under that system the priests and Levites were given forty-eight cities, spread throughout the land (Num. 35.7; Josh. 21.41). The area of each Levitical city was clearly defined: *"And ye shall measure from without the city on the east side two thousand cubits, and on the south side two thousand cubits, and on the west side two thousand cubits, and on the north side two thousand cubits; and the city shall be in the midst: this shall be to them the suburbs* [pasture land, RSV] *of the cities"* (Num. 35.5).

Converting these to current measurements, the area of each city and pasture land would have been a fraction over 1 km^2 (approximately 0.44 square miles, or 282 acres). Thus forty-eight cities would have given a total area for the priests and Levites of about 48 km^2 (21 square miles, 13,440 acres).

But Ezekiel was told that the total future allocation for both groups will be 25,000 x 20,000 cubits, in modern measurements 13.3 km x 10.7 km (8.29 miles x 6.62 miles), giving an area of 142 km^2 (54.8 square miles, or 35,072 acres). Thus it can be seen that the total future provision for the tribe of Levi will be almost three times that under the Law.

The city

The final component of the holy oblation is a strip of land adjoining that of the Levites, which contains a city, on either side of which will be farmland: *"The five thousand cubits in width that remain, along the edge of the twenty-five thousand, shall be for general use by the city, for dwellings and common-land; and the city shall be in the center"* (48.15, NKJV). The KJV translates the Hebrew for *"general use"* as *"profane"*, which to us may give the idea of some blasphemous connection. But according to Gesenius, it simply means "common" as opposed to "holy".

So, in contrast to the "most holy" area for the priests and the "holy" area of the Levites, this narrower area will be for general use – for the *"whole house of Israel"* (45.6). In the centre of the strip will be a city 4500 cubits square, with a 250 cubit open space all round it (48.15–17). In modern measurements the city will be 2.4 km (1.5 miles) square, with an area of nearly 6 km² (2.25 square miles, 1440 acres). It will have twelve gates, three on each side, spaced about 800 metres (500 yards) apart. Each gate will bear the name of a tribe of Israel; but, as with the allocation of the tribal portions considered in the previous chapter, it is difficult to see the significance of the order of the names.

The 5000 x 10,000 remainder on each side of the city (14.3 km², 5.5 square miles, 3500 acres) will be farmland whose *"produce shall be food for the workers of the city"* (v.18, NKJV). These workers in the city will be from *"all the tribes of Israel"* (v.19).

The role of the city

What is the purpose and function of this new city? No explicit information is given and, as in so many prophecies of the future, we can only make tentative suggestions. The new city will be in addition to Jerusalem, which will contain the temple. This, as mentioned before, will be the dwelling place of God on earth. So, why another city? There are some clues as to its purpose.

As well as providing a centre of worship and sacrifice for the *"people of the land"* (Ezek. 45.16, etc.), God's sanctuary will also be the place to which all nations will come and worship, as the following passages testify:

"All nations whom thou hast made shall come and worship before thee, O Lord; and shall glorify thy name" (Psa. 86.9).

"And it shall come to pass in the last days, that the mountain of the LORD'S house shall be established in the top of the mountains, and shall be exalted above the hills; and all nations shall flow unto it. And many people shall go and say, Come ye, and let us go up to the mountain of the LORD, to the house of the God of Jacob; and he will teach us of his ways,

and we will walk in his paths: for out of Zion shall go forth the law, and the word of the LORD from Jerusalem" (Isa. 2.2–3).

"At that time they shall call Jerusalem the throne of the LORD; and all the nations shall be gathered unto it, to the name of the LORD, to Jerusalem: neither shall they walk any more after the imagination of their evil heart" (Jer. 3.17).

So we can imagine that in the Kingdom there will be a regular, but presumably carefully timetabled, stream of visitors arriving in the Holy Land with the object of learning about God's ways and worshipping Him in the temple. They will need accommodation prior to their final ascent to the *"mountain of the LORD"* and this may be the function of the new city.

Who will be their instructors to teach them of God's ways? The immortal saints will no doubt have an input. They are the wise of whom Daniel speaks that *"turn many to righteousness"* (12.3), and we all can look forward to this great and satisfying work of explaining God's ways to a now receptive audience.

But it is possible that the Levites, through whose territory the pilgrims will have to pass on their way to the temple, will also have a role. This was part of their duties in the past (Deut. 33.10, etc.) and will be a means of emphasising the exalted status of the Jews as God's premier people in the future: *"In those days it shall come to pass, that ten men shall take hold out of all languages of the nations, even shall take hold of the skirt of him that is a Jew, saying, We will go with you: for we have heard that God is with you"* (Zech. 8.23).

"Yahweh shammah"

The suggestion that the new city will be the final staging-post before a pilgrim's ascent to Jerusalem is possibly confirmed by its designation. It is significant that the concluding statement concerning the temple is: *"The name of the city from that day shall be, The LORD is there"* (Ezek. 48.35). In Hebrew this name is *Yahweh shammah,* from which arises an interesting thought. *"The LORD is there"* is a legitimate translation but, as already noted, God had said that His dwelling place would be in the temple at Jerusalem, in the priestly area of the holy oblation: *"And he said unto me, Son of man, the place of my throne, and the place of the soles of my feet, where I will dwell in the midst of the children of Israel for ever"* (Ezek. 43.7). Why would another city be designated as God's dwelling?

The answer may lie in an alternative translation of *shammah.* This sometimes means "there", but is also translated *"from thence"* (Gen. 11.8), *"thither"* (Deut. 1.37), or *"whither"*: all implying journeying to a new location. We feel that Psalm 122 – a picture of the future – is especially relevant here as it describes pilgrimages to Jerusalem: *"Our feet shall stand within thy gates, O Jerusalem. Jerusalem is builded as a city that is compact together:* **whither** [Heb. *shammah*] *the tribes go up, the tribes of the LORD, unto the testimony of Israel, to give thanks unto the name of the LORD. For there are set thrones of judgement, the thrones of the house of David"* (Psa. 122.2–5). Thus Yahweh shammah can, and perhaps should, mean "Yahweh from thence"; meaning that it is from the new city that the pilgrims will set out on their journey up to Jerusalem, to God's dwelling place in the temple.

A progressive approach to God

What transpired from a detailed consideration of these arrangements, was the continuation of the teaching inherent in the approach to God as depicted in the tabernacle and the earlier temple. Our standard understanding of those ordinances is that God, in symbol dwelling in the tabernacle's most holy place, could only be approached by a process that gradually allowed an unclean, sinful person into God's presence by way of a set procedure. This in symbol entailed leaving the outside world, going through a single entrance, entering the holy place, with the prospect of then going further into the symbolic most holy place after the inhibiting veil of mortal flesh had been removed.

It seems that the future arrangements will have the same basic symbology. Any, Jew or Gentile, seeking to come to God must approach in a strictly defined way. First by way of the city, Yahweh shammah, in the "common" area; then into the Levites' portion, termed the "holy place"; and so into the "most holy" priestly area to visit the actual dwelling place of God on earth. Thus this literal journey will have the same spiritual teaching as did the tabernacle in the past.

As we conclude this study of the future temple, we hope that it has given a wonderful, even though inevitably imperfect, insight into the time when the blessings of Christ's reign will spread out into the whole world. Then all people will desire to render to their Creator the reverence and worship that is His due.

But true Christians are related to a more lasting divine dwelling place – a spiritual one. God's true temple is not one made with hands but consists of the perfected community of believers: *"in whom all the building fitly framed together groweth unto an holy temple in the Lord: in whom ye also are builded together for an habitation of God through the Spirit"* (Eph. 2.21–22).

It is our earnest prayer that each of our readers will share in that perfect and eternal fellowship.